THE ILLUSTRATED HISTORY OF THE
Third Reich

JOHN BRADLEY

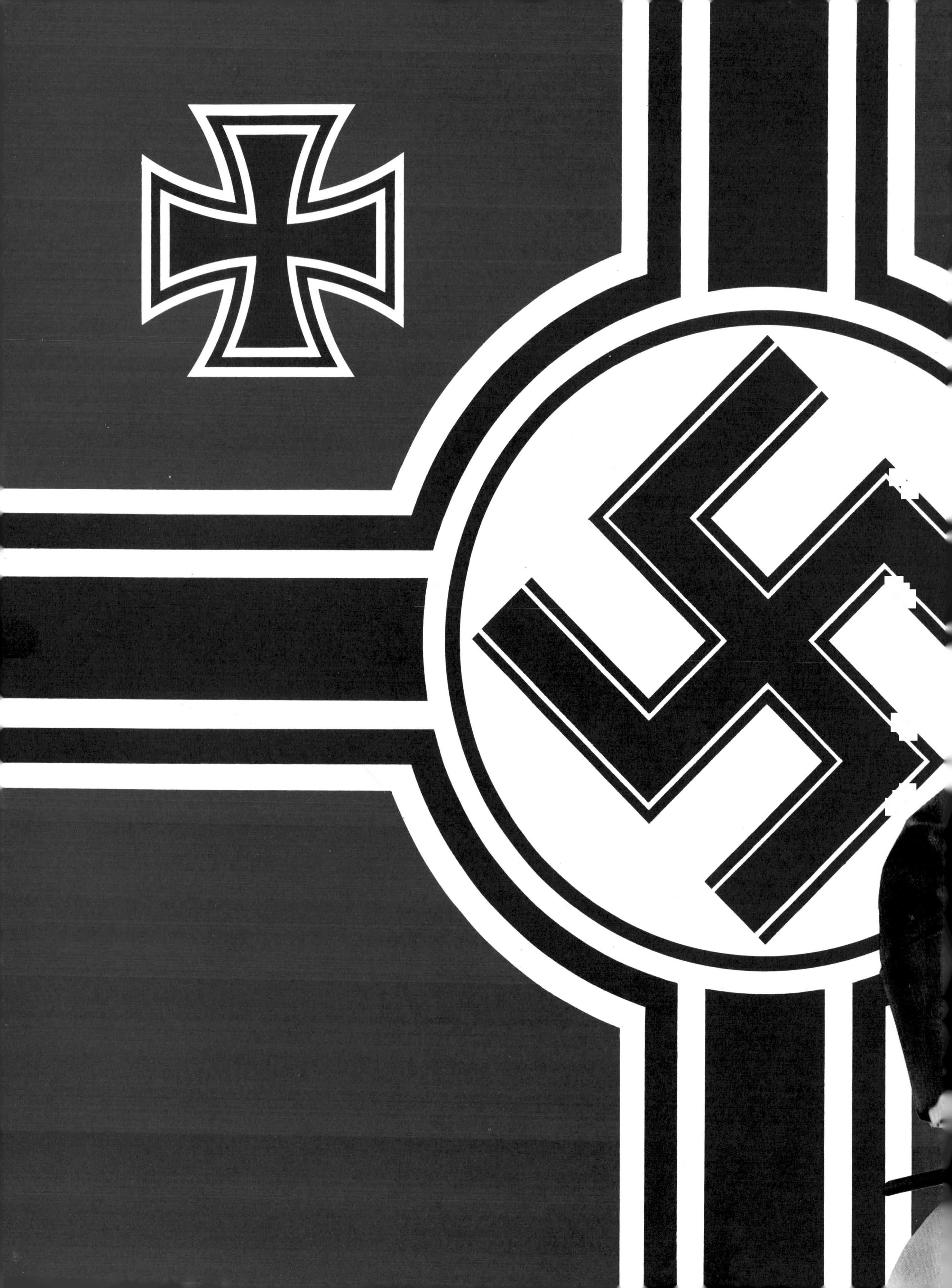

THE ILLUSTRATED HISTORY OF THE Third Reich

JOHN BRADLEY

Bison Books Limited

ISBN: 0-86124-013-8
Published by Bison Books Limited
4 Cromwell Place, London SW7

Printed in Japan

CONTENTS

THE YEARS OF HOPE

THE DISSOLUTION OF THE HOHENZOLLERN EMPIRE

Although William II, Emperor of Germany, always claimed that he did much to avoid the war and undoubtedly felt justified in his claim, both he and the German people went to war with enthusiasm. Right up to August 1918 Germans endured the victories and defeats of four years of war with equanimity. Although all the combatants wanted a short war, there had been no decisive outcome in 1914. The Germans had to fight on two fronts. In the West they were probably robbed of a decisive victory because of the questionable decision of a young Lieutenant Colonel called Hentsch, dispatched to the Front by the Chief of the General Staff, Moltke, to halt the offensive and retreat to the Aisne.

However in 1915 and 1916 Germany experienced many successes and reverses: in 1915 it was instrumental in humbling the Russian armies in the East; in 1916 the Russians administered a terrible rebuff. In the same year Serbia and Rumania were practically knocked out of the war, while in the West the trench warfare dragged on. In 1917 Russia finally dropped out, but the United States of America entered the war thanks to the Germans' desperate decision to wage unlimited naval warfare to defeat Great Britain. Despite this setback the year 1918 augured well: in March and May Germany signed separate peace treaties with Soviet Russia and Rumania, and transferred all her available forces from the East to effect a decisive push in the West. The war on two fronts came to an end and Erich Ludendorff's spring offensive brought German armies to within 40 miles of Paris. In the early summer of 1918 Emperor William and the German people thought themselves within sight of victory when suddenly disaster struck.

The whole German nation was intoxicated with the war and its leaders did not discern the danger signs as they appeared: in January 1918 400,000 Berlin workers went on strike, followed by over a million workers in other cities. The strikers wanted the democratization of government in Germany and peace without annexations. Foreign Minister von Kühlmann was dismissed abruptly when he voiced his doubts about the offensives in the West, but his dismissal did not stop American reinforcements arriving in France. In July the Allies launched their counterattacks and on 8 August 1918, the "Black Day of the Ger-

Below: **Gustav Noske addresses sailors involved in the Kiel Mutiny on 7 November 1918, which began the rising leading to the overthrow of the Kaiser on 9 November.**
Bottom: **Representatives of the Entente Allies inspect naval installations at Wilhelmshaven after the German surrender on 11 November 1918.**

Brüder!
Nicht schiessen!

Above : **German housewives in a bread line during the inflation of 1923.**
Top : **Berlin newspaper announces the new dollar-mark exchange rate of 1 : 1 million. It rose to four billion to the dollar before the mark was stabilized.**

Above left: **French Red Cross waiting room at Limburg station after the Ruhr occupation in 1923.**
Above: **Hitler and Ludendorff in a faked photograph, the two "leaders" of the Beer Hall Putsch.**
Left: **The fate of tens of thousands of unemployed and indigent Germans in the inflation crisis of 1923.**

Throughout these five years the country was governed by bourgeois coalitions which made Germany economically prosperous and internationally recognized. Stresemann, who served throughout as Foreign Minister, signed the Treaty of Locarno with the Allies. Germany was admitted into the community of great powers and subsequently into the League of Nations. Foreign investments poured into the country so that it could not only pay reparations but could also prosper itself. In 1925 the Founder-President, Ebert, died of appendicitis and Field Marshal Paul von Hindenburg was elected President; this was supposed to be the final sign of political stabilization. It is true that in the field of creative arts Germany became the world leader: Max Reinhardt produced his operas and theater plays, Walter Gropius's Bauhaus prospered while Fritz Lang among others experimented in film making. Paul Klee and Wassily Kandinsky painted in Germany; Berthold Brecht and a whole pleiad of writers flooded Germany with their left-wing creations. However there was another side to this picture of prosperity – the wholesale moral relaxation in Germany. People felt for the first time that the war was over, that austerity was a thing of the past and they let themselves go. This *joie de vivre* was somewhat negative. All sorts

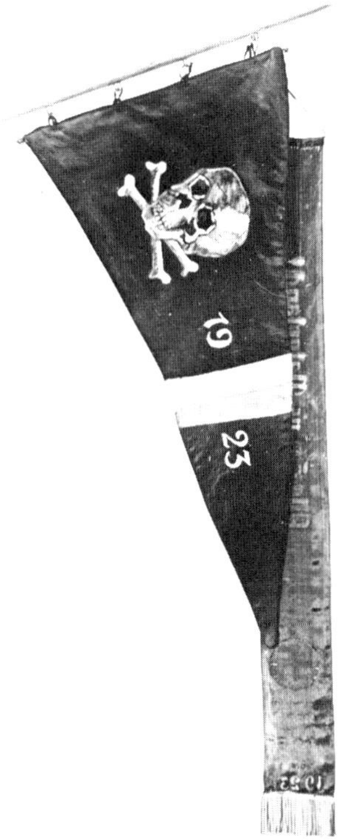

Above left : **An early SA flag of 1923.**
Above : **The Sterneckerbräu beer hall in Munich where the Nazi Party held its first public meetings. The Hofbräuhaus was also used.**
Left : **Members of the SA in the streets of Neustadt before the Beer Hall Putsch.**
Below : **The exterior of the beer hall in which the Nazi Party was founded.**

of vulgar entertainments sprang up, sexual perversions were in vogue, so that Germany lived out its "permissive" period in the 1920s, while Western Europe had to wait until the 1960s to reach it on the same scale. This permissive atmosphere failed to produce any real leaders, but rather catered for firebrand-miracle workers of Hitler's type. Moreover the first shock of the world depression shattered this perverted dream world and the brutal miracle worker, Hitler, was able to take over without any struggle at all.

There were no obvious indications of the deep crisis which immediately pre-

Left: **The second headquarters of the Nazi Party on the Corneliusstrasse 12 in Munich. The central organization was still funded solely by members' dues.**

ceded the demise of the Weimar Republic. On 29 May 1928 the Social Democrats won a handsome majority in the general election, while the Center only suffered marginal losses. Coalition government continued, though the Communists increased their representation (from 45 seats in 1924 to 54) and the Nazis, for the first time, won national representation in the Reichstag: they polled 810,000 votes and obtained a modest 12 seats. Then suddenly in 1929, after the collapse of the New York Stock Exchange, Germany itself was hit: American investors, who formed the bulk of the foreigners who had financed the five year boom, began to call in the short term loans which they had made in Germany. As a result banks began to collapse and many businesses went bank-

Right: **The SA in 1922.**
Below: **A Nazi Party meeting in Oberwiesenfeld in May 1923; some are wearing *Freikorps* uniforms.**

Above : **Hitler soon after he became a Nazi in 1921.**
Right : **Hitler, one of the many faces in the crowd, watching a parade of Nazis on German Day in Munich in 1923.**
Below : **Nazi rally in Oberwiesenfeld, 1 May 1923.**

rupt. However, the most severe blow was felt in the sphere of employment: by 1930 Germany had 3 million unemployed and their number doubled by 1932. Germany's economy was shattered and lay in ruin, with far-reaching repercussions in politics which overnight became polarized and radicalized; the most spectacular was the electoral rise of the Nazi Party. Compared to 1928 they polled 6.5 million votes in September 1930 (107 seats) and almost doubled their strength in July 1932, when they obtained 230 seats and became the strongest party in the Reichstag.

Thus it took Hitler, who was throughout the leader (Führer) of the National Socialist Workers' Party, twelve years to arrive at the gates of supreme power in the Weimar Republic, and considering the humble beginnings and reverses that Hitler and the party suffered in these twelve years, it was a remarkable feat. On closer examination the miraculous aspect of Hitler's progress becomes more comprehensible when the total irresponsibility and gray inability of the Weimar politicians is taken into account. From the very beginning Hitler and his movement hovered on the extreme nationalist right and made its way up in the political arena on the back of the conservatives. On the other hand, to arrive where it did in 1932, Hitler and the Nazis had to attract to themselves the disaffected working class voters; in this way they obtained real electoral substance, but this took them some ten years to achieve.

As was the case with all the extremist movements and parties, the year 1923 was for the Nazis a fateful landmark. In Bavaria the mood was one of defiance of the central government bordering on rebellion, and Hitler rather ill-advisedly decided to exploit it. In 1923 Hitler's party was not distinguished by its electoral strength but by the oratory of its leader and the organization and toughness of its orderlies, the so-called *Sturm Abteilung* – Storm Troopers. In September 1923 Hitler formed a coalition with other extremist Bavarian organizations, the *Deutscher Kampfbund*, and this made the SA feel that they could seize power in Bavaria provided Hitler smoothed over matters with the "rebellious" authorities. On 26 September 1923 Premier Eugen von Knilling proclaimed a state of emergency in Bavaria and handed over power to the

Below: **Nazis erect barricades in Munich in front of the War Ministry during the Beer Hall *Putsch* of 9 November 1923. Only 3000 people joined Hitler and the *Putsch* flopped badly.**

former Premier, Gustav von Kahr, whom he made a Reichscommissioner. Kahr confirmed General Otto Hermann von Lossow, the sacked Bavarian commander of the *Reichswehr*, as commanding officer and with the aid of the Police Colonel Hans von Seisser the triumvirate continued to govern Bavaria in defiance of Berlin. Then Hitler decided to force the triumvirate into an open rebellion against the Reich government, march on Berlin and seize power.

However, this time Hitler's calculations went awry. After he had tried to seize power locally with his SA, who were ready all round Munich to storm the city (provided the police and the *Reichswehr* did not oppose them), Hitler had finally seized his last opportunity on the evening of 8 November when the triumvirate gathered at a public meeting in the Bürgerbräukeller (a famous beer hall) to spark off the takeover throughout Germany. While Hitler dramatically burst into the beer hall and announced to the Assembly that power was theirs, he failed to impress the triumvirate with his Iron Cross and the spiked helmet which he wore together with a tuxedo; they left the beer hall as soon as they could and took different dispositions from those of Hitler. The commissioner patched up a compromise with Berlin; the general declared the Army neutral and the police commissioner dispatched his security forces to a few strategic places in the city. In the morning, when Hitler with his SA and a large following (some 3000) tried to march and take over the city, one volley from the police put a stop to his deadly comedy. The crowd dispersed in panic, Hitler disappeared and went into hiding, while only the former Chief of the Imperial Staff, General Ludendorff, marched on and was finally arrested by the police.

Hitler's *Putsch* collapsed quickly and though the Nazi leaders scattered – Her-

Far left and left: **These men who fell during the Beer Hall *Putsch* were honored by the Nazis.**
Below: **SA troops enter Munich for the *Putsch* on 9 November 1923.**

Left: **Julius Streicher addresses the reorganized Nazi Party in Weimar in 1926.**
Above: **Ritter von Epp, a Bavarian war hero, who was an early supporter of the Nazi Party.**

Above: **Hitler in Landsberg Prison where he wrote *Mein Kampf*. His oration at the time of his sentencing is printed on the left.**

mann Goering and Rudolf Hess fled to Austria – they were all arrested together with Hitler in his hiding place at Uffing, and on 24 February 1924 they were put on trial in Munich. Paradoxically this show trial served to turn Hitler's defeat into a triumph. Of the ten accused (among whom was Ludendorff) Hitler was easily the greatest orator and propagandist, and he quickly made the prosecuting authorities look as guilty as the accused. Hitler's

Below: **Hitler and one of the Strasser brothers after his release from prison.**

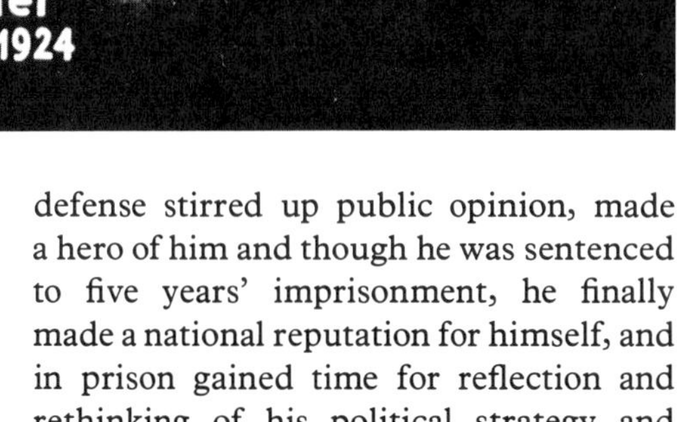

defense stirred up public opinion, made a hero of him and though he was sentenced to five years' imprisonment, he finally made a national reputation for himself, and in prison gained time for reflection and rethinking of his political strategy and tactics.

Hitler's sentence and imprisonment were not as harsh as they appeared at first sight. He served only nine months of the sentence and then was freed. While in the old Landsberg prison-fortress, he was treated as an honored guest and not as a prisoner. He was surrounded by his fellow Nazis, was allowed any number of visitors, continued to run the party from prison and in fact dictated his propaganda memoirs, *Mein Kampf*, while at Landsberg. Although *Mein Kampf* became the bible of nazism and surprisingly contained all Hitler's political ideas for the future, it was not taken seriously at all when it came out in the fall of 1925. Not surprisingly, the book was written in rather turgid style – a jumble of half-baked ideas, trends and moods. Politically it was nothing but opportunism with the underlying will to power. The three pillars of Hitler's views were nationalism, anti-Bolshevism and anti-Semitism. While in prison Hitler had read a number of books on Darwinism and the philosophy of history. He immediately incorporated these ideas into his book: the future for him was a titanic struggle for the survival of the fittest: the iron laws of nature were used to excuse brutality, ruthlessness and a complete disregard for the rights of individuals. Such struggle then was necessary to arrest the decay of the Aryan (Germanic) race which he conceived (borrowing heavily from

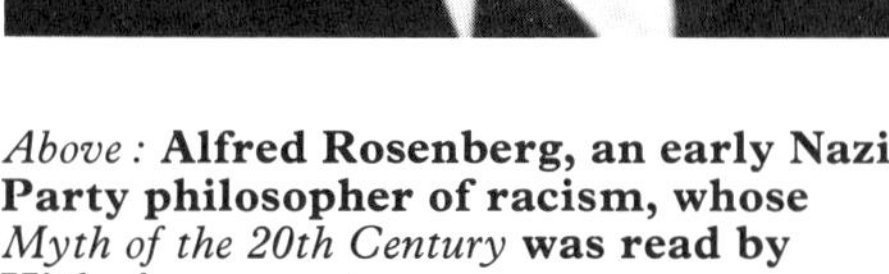

Above: **Alfred Rosenberg, an early Nazi Party philosopher of racism, whose *Myth of the 20th Century* was read by Hitler's supporters.**

Gobineau) as superior: the decay of this superior race was the responsibility of the Jews and they had to be wiped out before the thousand-year Germanic Reich could be established on earth. The triumph of the Germanic race would be brought about only if the German nation would forsake its imperfect democracy and become united under a leader (Führer) and for this rôle he proposed himself. Hitler's imprisonment and ideological ruminations therein had two significant political results: the Nazis would never again attempt a *putsch* and would at any cost come to power "legally," observing the principles which Hitler lay down for political success: unity under one leader, vigorous opportunistic propaganda and making maximum use of the democratic means that were available. Still the road to power was long and difficult.

While in prison Hitler resigned the leadership of the Nazi party and when he emerged from Landsberg found the party in ruin. Perhaps a little fortunately for Hitler no rival Führer arose from this moribund body politic, so he could smoothly regain the leadership and start anew. Within two weeks of his release Hitler had an interview with the Bavarian Premier, Heinrich Held, and promised him that he would continue his political struggle on a strictly legal basis. Shortly afterwards, the ban on the Nazi party was lifted and it was allowed to hold public meetings and publish a newspaper: the *Völkischer Beobachter* re-appeared on 26 February 1925. How-

Left : **Hitler in a series of posed shots of his orating posture in the mid-1920s.**
Above : **Hitler honors those Nazis who died in the 1920s.**
Below : **Hitler, with Brückner, Dr Frick, Sauckel and Hierl in Weimar during a rally in 1931.**

ever, Hitler was still out of prison on probation and so had to keep in the background; nevertheless he could continue to re-organize the party according to the ideas he had formulated in Landsberg. Since no one of significance wanted to put these principles into practice, Hitler practically broke with every "reputable" Nazi: Ludendorff, Ehrhardt, Streicher, and Röhm. However, Gregor Strasser remained by him and with his aid Hitler succeeded in remolding the party into his personal instrument of power. Röhm's defection also meant that the SA had to be re-organized according to Hitler's wishes and became firmly subordinate to the political leadership. Nevertheless the SA remained an unreliable instrument and Hitler formed a special bodyguard unit, the SS (*Schütz Staffel*). By 1928 when the Nazis once again fought an election their party membership amounted to some 150,000 and they polled some 2.6 percent of the vote, a clear indication of weakness but also a sign of revival, when compared to the catastrophe in 1924.

In 1929 Hitler and the renovated party at last made the break into national politics. Germany, struck by recession, once again had difficulties with reparations payments and the Young Plan which was to solve these problems was attacked by the German Nationalist right wing. The rather unsuccessful Nationalist leader, Alfred Hugenberg, proposed an alliance with Hitler's Nazis whom he thought he

Above: In the Beginning was the Word, **a stagey painting by H O Hoyer.**
Below: **Hitler with SA leader Victor Lutze on Party Day in Braunschweig in 1931.**

Below: **Hitler, Goebbels and Dietrich at the Berghof in Berchtesgaden.**

Left : **The march past of SA troops in Harzburg in 1931 is saluted by their Führer.**
Above : **Hitler addresses his radio public in 1932 during the election campaign of that year.**

Und Ihr habt doch gesiegt!
Daß wir das noch erleben konnten!
Wann werde ich den Führer sehen

Far left: **Nazi supporters explain why they back the Führer. The grandfather says it was in order to exist. The granddaughter asks when she will see the Führer.**
Left: **Hitler with Franzen and Dietrich Klegges, a local schoolteacher, in Braunschweig in February 1931.**
Below: **Unemployed gather in Hamburg near the docks after the Depression struck Germany in 1930.**
Below right: **Unemployed workers play cards to while away the time. Support from the lost millions of unemployed was the basis for Hitler's rise to power.**

could use. Although the newfangled alliance failed in its referendum bid on the Young Plan (it only got 14 percent of the electorate to vote against the Young Plan), for the first time it gave the Nazis access to propaganda means and they certainly put them to good use. The chain of newspapers controlled by Hugenberg gave Hitler free publicity; Hugenberg's name also added prestige to Hitler who was able to meet businessmen and industrialists, some of whom (Thyssen) began to support his party financially. Thus Emil Kirdorf established and administered for Hitler the Ruhr Treasury, a political fund which enabled Hitler to refurbish his Munich Headquarters, pay permanent party officials (*Gauleiteren*) and win for the first time a regional election (Wilhelm Frick became the first Nazi Land Premier).

Under the impact of the depression the Weimar Republic began to falter politically. From 1930 it moved from parliamentary to presidential government: the coalition government fell apart in the spring of 1930. The 82-year old President, Field Marshal Paul von Hindenburg, appointed as his Chancellor the Catholic Center leader, Heinrich Brüning, who was recommended to him by General Kurt von Schleicher of the *Reichswehr* and the President's *homme de confiance*. Brüning governed the country by virtue of emergency decrees signed by the President and ratified by the Reichstag. The Social Democrats supported this type of govern-

IA17402
ME MOUSON
Wähle deutschnational!

Top left: **Nazi supporters brandishing the deposed Kaiser's flag during the 1928 election campaign.**
Above: **Nazi supporters festoon the streets near Berlin's Brandenburg Gate with propaganda leaflets.**
Top right: **Propaganda leaflets of the German Peoples' Party are strewn during the election of 1924.**

Geschlossene Börsen.

Traurige Statistik
Immer mehr Selbstmorde

Bankenschluss.

Golddeckung 35,8 Prozent!

Gehaltszahlung in Raten

Lohnsenkung!

Notverordnung

Arbeitslosigkeit steigt

Owen Young, (below), author of the Young Plan of 1929 to continue to stabilize Germany's currency. The Depression which immediately followed it used the Plan as a cause for unemployment, as these headlines (left) showed: Unemployment rises, banks close, stock exchanges close, etc.

ment in the Reichstag, preferring it to an open right-wing dictatorship. However as soon as they disapproved of any of his measures (for example, the budget) Brüning dissolved the Reichstag and a new election took place which invariably failed to resolve the parliamentary impasse. In September 1930 the Nazis finally achieved their electoral breakthrough; although their election program was ridiculously superficial and naive – they accused France, the November traitors, marxists, freemasons, Jesuits and the Jews of ruining Germany – they nevertheless polled some 6,380,000 votes and had 107 deputies in the new Reichstag, thus making them the second largest party. Only the Social Democrats with their 143 seats beat the Nazis, while Chancellor Brüning's Center gained only 76 seats. Nonetheless the President re-appointed Brüning as Chancellor and he continued until 1932. It was evident that power was no longer in the Reichstag but rather in the President's Chancellery and in the streets and houses of the cities.

Economic depression obviously radicalized German politics and the sinking middle class flocked to the Nazi party. But they were not the only ones: the unemployed joined the SA in scores, while at universities the Nazi Students' Union made surprising headway. They controlled the universities at Erlangen, Jena, Rostock and Breslau. It seemed that elections served only as a pretext for street

Above left: **Hitler leaves the Clou Konzert Hall in Berlin after making an election speech there in 1932.**
Left: **Prussian Interior Minister Carl Severing leaves the polls after the first round of the Presidential election of 1932.**

Left: **Hitler with General Franz Ritter von Epp in 1929. Von Epp was an officer in the District Command in Munich and in March 1933 led a Nazi coup in Bavaria.**
Above: **Hitler in his SA cap in the same year, 1929.**
Below: **A rally in Gera in 1931 as the Nazi movement gathered momentum.**

Above left : **Hitler leaves a meeting in 1927.**
Below : **Hitler and SA Leader Ernst Röhm on Party Day in Nuremberg.**

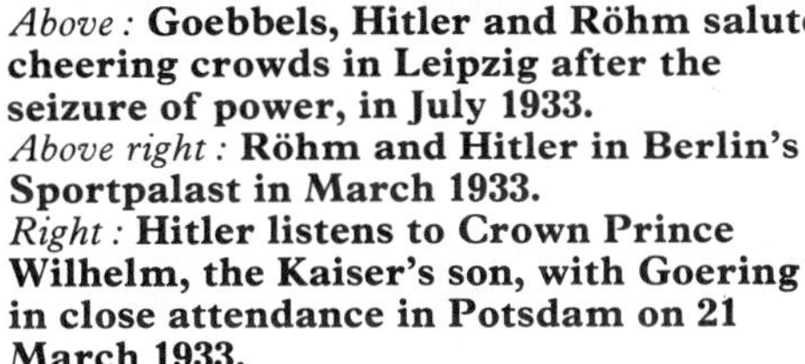

Above : **Goebbels, Hitler and Röhm salute cheering crowds in Leipzig after the seizure of power, in July 1933.**
Above right : **Röhm and Hitler in Berlin's Sportpalast in March 1933.**
Right : **Hitler listens to Crown Prince Wilhelm, the Kaiser's son, with Goering in close attendance in Potsdam on 21 March 1933.**

battles among rival parties, which all had their paramilitary organizations: the *Stahlhelm, Reichsbanner, Eiserne Republikanische Abwehr des Faschismus, Rote Front* and of course the SA which counted some 300,000 or 400,000 members. In 1932 the election result was so surprising that the Nazis simply did not have enough candidates to field (Hitler who was not a German citizen could not stand) and it caused the final economic collapse. Foreign investors fearing political upheavals pulled out of Germany altogether. Some of the Nazis, puffed up by their electoral triumph, wanted to seize power and Hitler had to calm them down. The Berlin SA became overexcited and rebelled against Hitler's leadership; in addition the party had to be purged of the Strasser brothers and their followers. However, Hitler sensed that power was coming his way: he continued to campaign vigorously and to prepare himself and his more loyal followers for the final "seizure" of power.

As in 1924, so in 1930 Hitler achieved national publicity during the trial for treason of three young Nazi officers. In the same year he needed the SA so he re-appointed Röhm to lead them and "prepare them for civil war." In 1931 when parliamentary immunity was lifted, the Nazis left the Reichstag and fought for power in the streets, registering some 50 dead martyrs in a year. Perhaps the greatest national notoriety was achieved by Hitler in the two rounds of presidential election in March and April 1932. On 13 March the old President was almost re-

Left : **Poster commemorating the 10th anniversary of the founding of the Nazi Students' League in 1936.**
Above : **A rally in Coburg in 1932 with stewards of the SA.**
Below left : **Goebbels arrives to a garlanded welcome at the grassy Königsberg airfield.**
Below : **Some of the 100,000 SA men who gathered at Nuremberg for Party Day.**

Left: **"If you save five marks a week, you can own your own car" says this poster urging the German public to save for their new Volkswagen.**
Above: **Poster rallying support for the Nazis from the whole family.**

temberg and Thuringia, while the mini-lands followed suit at the end of the month. Since Prussia was already under Goering's unconstitutional control, the German federation was in fact dissolved and the process which was called the *Gleichschaltung* (Streamlining) resulted in fact in the Nazification of these administrative units and historical states. Local Nazis – sometimes *Gauleiteren* – were appointed Governors with powers to dismiss and nominate civil servants and police officers. Next in the *Gleichschaltung* came the trade unions. The Catholic Trade Union leader, Stegerweld, was beaten up during the election campaign as well as many other lesser trade unionists. The violence exhibited by the SS and SA towards trade unionists prompted the Trade Union Congress Chairman, Theodor Leipart, to issue a letter of protest and an appeal for protection to the President. No protection came from the Head of State, but Nazi vengeance was swift. They had previously declared 1 May as the National Labor Day. It was celebrated by all and sundry without political distinction. However on 2 May the SA broke into and occupied all left-wing trade union offices, arrested their leaders and officials and sent most of them into concentration camps. In June 1933 Christian trade unions received the same treatment and the Nazis instead, created the German Labor Front. Both employers and employees were forced to join this front whose function was to conciliate rather than advance demands.

Once Hitler finished with the Reichstag he had no use for the parties of which it was composed. The Communist party was dissolved before the election and its elected deputies were put *en masse* into "protective custody" and sent to a concentration camp for the duration. On 22 June 1933 the Social Democratic party was dissolved as an anti-state, subversive body and its property confiscated. A week later the German Nationalist Party attracted the wrath of the SA by organizing its own paramilitary formations. When the SA moved against these Green Shirts, the Nationalist leader, Hugenberg, resigned from the government and the party dissolved itself. Early in July the Catholic Center went into voluntary liquidation, followed by the People's Party and Bavarian People's Party. Thereafter the government decreed (Act of 14 July 1933) that Germany was a One-Party state and the formation of any other party was judged a treasonable act punishable by imprisonment. The ease with which Hitler disposed of the trade unions and political parties conclusively proved how decayed these bodies must have become and how badly led they must have been.

Gleichschaltung was carried out not only in the power sphere but affected the whole of national life. As was usual with Hitler even racial *Gleichschaltung* was sanctioned by the law, albeit retrospectively. On 1 April 1933 the vitriolic anti-Semite Julius Streicher proclaimed a nation-wide boycott of Jewish shops and was most efficient-

Right: **"Mother and Child" was the slogan on this poster. The Nazis encouraged large families and paid bounties to those willing to have children.**

ly backed by gangs of SA men who enforced it. In response to these pressures some 235,000 Jews departed from Germany leaving the field of German science somewhat denuded. However in Germany Jews were expelled wholesale from all the liberal professions, be it medicine, law, journalism, fine arts, radio, cinema, music or civil service. Jewish university professors had their lectures disrupted by fanatical students and simply had to abandon their profession. Still the complex anti-Jewish legislation was passed only on 15 September 1935 (the Nuremberg Laws) and Jewish property was "legally" confiscated on 3 December 1938. From the very beginning the Jews were subjected to naked terror which increased with time (Crystal Night 1938), until it culminated in the "final solution" in 1941 when they were to be all physically liquidated.

Only with the Communists was Hitler prepared to go as far as with the Jews, but even with them the *Gleichschaltung*-liquidation was applied gradually so as not to alarm domestic or international public opinion. The ultimate fate of the Christian Churches would probably have been the same as that of the Jews and Communists. During the war Alfred Rosenberg made it clear when he drew up the National Reich Church Program which proposed to replace the Bible by *Mein Kampf* and the Cross by the swastika – only a few rites were to be retained albeit in adapted form. The Catholic Church, which on the whole resisted the Nazis more successfully than the Protestant Churches, was treated with disdain. When Schulze, Cardinal-Archbishop of Cologne, protested against SA and SS brutalities in 1933, he was ignored. On 20 July 1933 Hitler signed a Concordat with the Vatican and immediately broke it: arrests of priests and nuns continued unabated, while many Catholic laymen found themselves in the numerous concentration camps. By 14 March 1937, Pius XI openly lamented the state of the Church in Nazi Germany.

With the Protestant Churches, which were disunited, the damage inflicted by the Nazis was immeasurably greater. In 1933 the Conference of Protestant Churches was declared illegal and the German Christians, a group of some 3000 pastors

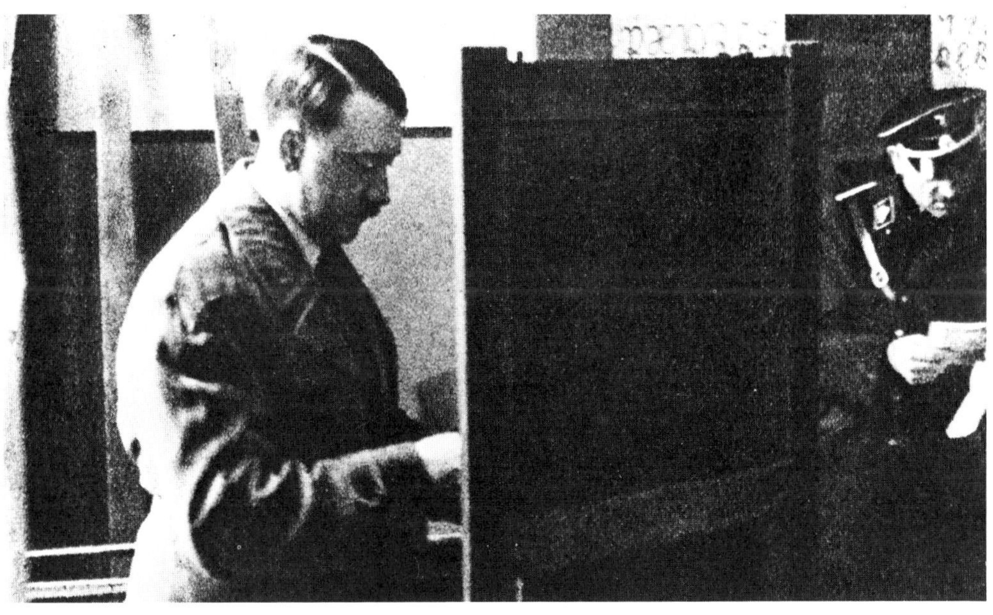

Right: **Hitler votes in Königsberg in the election of April 1933. On the right is Sepp Dietrich, his personal bodyguard, who became an SS General and commanded the Sixth Panzer Army during World War II.**

Left: **SA members bear the Kaiser's flag as late as 1933.**
Above: **"All Germany Listens to the Führer" was the slogan on this poster.**
Above center: **"Workers Choose the Front Soldier Hitler."**
Above right: **Women with unemployed husbands and hungry children were encouraged to vote for Hitler with this poster.**

(out of 17,000), were encouraged to take over; this was supposed to be a church *Gleichschaltung*. While the German Christians supported Nazi racial policies only, another group, the Confessional Church wanted to go the whole way and support the Nazis in everything. They argued that Luther was not only a Jew-hater but also an upholder of political power; since power was now in the hands of the Nazis they had to be supported. Soon, however, the Nazis and their sympathizers overreached themselves when they wanted to impose on the synod gathered at Wittenberg a new Reich bishop. Pastor Martin Niemöller, formerly a German Christian, formed a resistance group which gradually neutralized the other factions. By 1937 the Protestant Churches began a process of re-unification and the Nazis arrested and imprisoned not only Niemöller but over 800 pastors as well. By the spring of 1938 most of the remaining clergy swore allegiance to Hitler and the Protestants were deemed "co-ordinated."

In the sphere of culture the *Gleichschaltung* was instant. On 10 May 1933 bonfires were started with proscribed books of anti-Nazi writers. In September 1933 the Reichs Chamber of Culture was set up under the new Minister of Propaganda, Dr Goebbels, and henceforth all manuscripts had to be submitted to the ministry before they could be published. As a result almost all the writers of any standing emigrated and Germany was left with party hacks whose works were foisted on the public – at this time Hitler's *Mein Kampf* finally sold in millions and he became a writer-millionaire, which was rare in Germany. Although composers were much less bullied they were forced to sever all relations with Jewish and anti-Nazi friends; otherwise they found themselves unperformed. In fine arts in which Hitler took a personal interest some 6500 "decadent" paintings were removed from German museums and art galleries. Later on Hitler personally selected German paintings which were exhibited in the House of German Art in Munich but attendance was low. On the contrary the Ministry of Propaganda's exhibition of "degenerate" art proved so embarrassingly popular that it had to be closed down.

The left-wing press was suppressed even before the March election; when Goebbels set up his Propaganda Ministry all the newspapers were published under the auspices of this Ministry: daily instructions supplemented by oral orders were issued. After 230 years the *Vössische Zeitung* closed down as it found it impos-

Right: **Goebbels leaves a polling station in Berlin after voting in the 1933 election. The posters proclaim "Führer, We Follow Thee."**

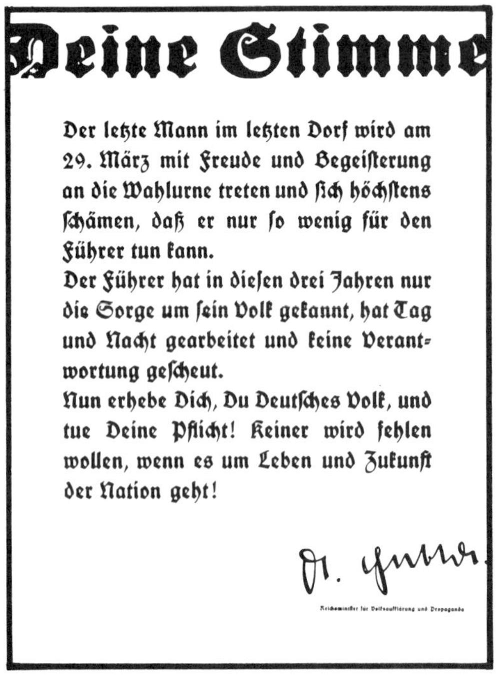

Deine Stimme

Der letzte Mann im letzten Dorf wird am 29. März mit Freude und Begeisterung an die Wahlurne treten und sich höchstens schämen, daß er nur so wenig für den Führer tun kann.

Der Führer hat in diesen drei Jahren nur die Sorge um sein Volk gekannt, hat Tag und Nacht gearbeitet und keine Verantwortung gescheut.

Nun erhebe Dich, Du Deutsches Volk, und tue Deine Pflicht! Keiner wird fehlen wollen, wenn es um Leben und Zukunft der Nation geht!

Dr. Goebbels

Reichsminister für Volksaufklärung und Propaganda

Above : **Poster signed by Goebbels tells Germans that it is their duty to support Hitler in the 1935 election.**
Right : **Goering, Darré, Hitler and Krause at a rally in Bückeburg in 1934.**

sible to work in such conditions. As newspapers became "co-ordinated" and their contents hardly differed from that of the official party newspapers *Völkischer Beobachter*, their circulation steeply declined and they went bankrupt. Subsequently they were bought by the giant party publishing house, the *Eher Verlag*, and the party enjoyed a practical monopoly of the press.

In education, although purges were immediately put in hand, the Nazis tried to implement long-term policies. Bernhard Rust, the teacher-*Gauleiter*, became Reichsminister of science, education and popular culture and immediately ordered all textbooks to be re-written in the Nazi spirit; overnight he had changed school and university curricula. However the teaching profession was hardly touched by the Nazis – after the initial expulsion of Jewish and left-wing elements – and faithfully served the Nazis throughout their reign. Professors of medicine became particularly compromised – some of them serving not as savers of life but exterminators of the feeble, incurable and "inferior" races (Gypsies, Jews). Hardly anyone opposed the Nazis who ordered these abject timeservers to invent Germanic physics, mathematics, jurisprudence and even natural sciences. In 1937 the Civil Service Act made the teaching profession the executor of the will of the Party-state and the perilous state of education was exemplified by the halving of the student population in the six years that followed the Nazis' seizure of power.

In youth organization the *Gleichschaltung* meant a wholesale takeover of all youth organization by the Nazi youth movement, the *Hitler Jugend*; the half-American Baldur von Schirach became its leader. The Nazis seized the national offices of the Youth Association and dissolved the Catholic Youth Association; the rest were incorporated into the *Hitler Jugend*. By 1938 the *Hitler Jugend* amounted to some 7 million members; since some 4 million young people stayed out of this organization, its membership became compulsory. All youth, boys and girls between 6–18

Above: **Hitler queries Dr Todt about the construction of the autobahn while Hitler's aides Krause and Brückner listen intently.**
Below: **Hitler inspects the new section of the Leipzig autobahn which represented over 1000 miles of motorway constructed by 1937.**

Above left : **Hitler inaugurates the construction of the autobahn in 1933 as Julius Streicher, Dr Todt, whose** *Organisation Todt* **supervized construction, and Dr Ley observe.**
Above : **Architectural design for Berlin at Munich's House of German Art in 1938.**
Left : **Model for the entrance to the autobahn near Salzburg on the Austrian border.**

had to join and were organized in a para-military manner, indoctrinated and marched up and down Germany. The results of this youthful indoctrination are incalculable even nowadays.

In the economic sphere the Nazis, owing to Hitler's own confusion, did not have the least idea how to create a boom. Here Hitler had the good fortune of reaping the results of measures taken by his predecessors, Brüning and Papen, and of putting in charge of the economy an experienced expert, Dr Schacht. Still the resulting economic order was somewhat new and the Nazis claimed uniquely their own. Thus no nationalizations were operated in Germany, but the capitalists lost their freedom of investment and fixing prices and wages. In addition Dr Schacht proclaimed two four-year economic plans, one to run from 1933–7 whose aim was to revive the economy and eliminate unemployment. The second was to run from 1937 to 1941 by which time Germany was to achieve autarky. In effect Dr Schacht began to revive the economy by large-scale public works (prepared by Brüning and put into effect by Papen). Schacht's original contribution was the way in which he financed the program: he issued special bills of exchange repayable in five years and easily achieved his objectives. While in 1933 there were six million unemployed, in 1935 there was one million left and by

1939 there was a labor shortage. To start with, the unemployed were put into the *Arbeitsdienst* (Labor Service) and they began to build a new system of expressways. Subsequently Schacht had it easy because the Nazis cowed trade unions; he could direct labor wherever it was needed and had wages and prices under his control. The economy was also helped by the re-introduction of military service, expansion of the civil service and party administration, while women vacated many jobs when they began to get increased family allowances. Although there were large investments in equipment, the fastest expanding sector of the economy became the armament industry, for Hitler immediately rejected the Versailles Treaty limitations. Naturally a lot of money had to be printed, but with import restrictions and confiscation of Jewish capital the first four-year plan was a success. However from the very beginning in 1933, this was a war economy, which some argue, inevitably led to war: therefore in political terms the economic success was reversed. During the second four-year plan (Schacht resigned in 1937 and was replaced by a party hack, Walter Funk) serious failures became apparent; still by 1939 Germany was better prepared for war than any of its enemies, whose economies, either capitalist or Communist, did not undergo the Nazi treatment.

In agriculture the Nazis proved inconsistent and even less successful than in industry. In 1933 farmers solidly backed the Nazis after a decade of slump, but when Walter Darré became Minister of Agriculture and began to exercise pressure in favor of the agricultural interests coming down, he was promptly silenced by Hitler and the Nazis never touched that problem again, although loan repayments were most oppressive and amounted to some 14 percent of the farmers' income. The Nazis also failed to distribute land to smallholders leaving the large feudal estates intact. Darré did enact two useful laws: one prevented further division of land (Hereditary Farm Act) and the other regulated farm production (Reich Food Estate Act). But after the numerous promises that he had made to the farmers his achievements were minor indeed. Although agricultural production aimed at self-sufficiency, Germany by 1938 still depended on imports (some 17 percent of its consumption).

The Nazification of the government was the smoothest of all. On 14 March 1933 Hitler named his new cabinet, and he retained all the non-Nazi ministers, as he

Above: **Hitler proudly points out aspects of his model of Berlin, with Heinz Hoffman and Robert Ley on the Führer's left.**

Below: **Hitler gloats over his model of Berlin in 1938 in the presence of an Italian general, Altolico, and an architect, Dr Dolmetscher.**

Above: **Hitler and Röhm study a document a few months before Hitler gave the order to have him purged. Röhm was shot by two SS men.**
Left: **Munich's Königsplatz was the scene of a Nazi rally commemorating the Beer Hall** ***Putsch*** **on 9 November 1935.**

had promised, particularly to Hugenberg. The only addition seemed Dr Goebbels who headed a new Ministry of Propaganda and Culture. Significantly Papen, although he retained the Vice-Chancellorship, lost the *Reichskommissariat* of Prussia. Hitler made himself *Reichsstatthalter* of Prussia; he then delegated all powers to Goering. The Nazis were formally in charge of the most important state which Goering properly Nazified. In 1933 it was still unclear how this "nationalist" coalition would work, and Hitler only made it clear after June-July 1934. As it was, he did not need the President, since he had full powers to rule by decree himself, and he only rarely bothered to see him. Since he conceived the full powers as being given by the Reichstag to him personally, he not only dispensed with the Reichstag, but also with individual Ministers. After all it was the Nazi Party backed by the crude force of the SA and SS which was running everything in Germany, so why should Hitler trouble himself about his political allies? The government continued to meet erratically but no vote was taken on policies invariably announced by the Führer. In June 1933 Hitler had to get rid of Hugenberg who thought that the government should be run differently and also dared to protest to the President. Hugenberg's Ministries were handed over to the Nazis. Darré took over the Ministry of Food and Agriculture, while Dr Kurt Schmitt was given the Ministry of the Economy. Subsequently Gereke and Seldte were also dismissed and Hitler strengthened his hand in the government, lest he needed it, by appointing Rudolf Hess and Ernst Röhm as Ministers without Portfolio. If Hitler paid not the slightest attention to the ministers of his cabinet, the appointment of Röhm was nevertheless of great significance. Röhm, the Head of the SA, the thugs who were *de facto* Nazifying Germany, was left out of positions of power until December 1933. Throughout the summer of 1933 he complained about Hitler's *Machtergreifung und Evolution*, while he would have preferred *Revolution*. Since his SAs were doing most of the dirty work he wanted some recompense for his underpaid three millions. Above all he wanted their position regularized by having them included in the *Reichswehr* with corresponding ranks. Thus his appointment could only mean that he was intended to counter-balance the Minister of Defense, von Blomberg, and ultimately perhaps take over from him. In addition, the SA as a whole, while very busy enforcing the Nazification of Germany, mumbled increasingly loudly about the second revolution along socialist lines, so dear to Hitler in the early days of his movement.

Thus difficulties with Röhm and his SAs were the only real problem that Hitler encountered after coming to power: it could not be ignored and it would not go away as others had done. After much hesitation Hitler decided to solve the problem by force. The SA had always been turbulent, uncontrollable, mutinous and above all they began to irritate the only institution that Hitler wanted to leave intact and non-Nazified, the *Reichswehr*. By the end of 1933 violence was no longer needed from the SA and Hitler thought that Röhm would be satisfied with his ministerial position. For the time Röhm seemed content, but the SA as a whole continued to voice ideas about a real Socialist revolution. The objects of their hatred were threefold: the middle class,

Above: **Ernst Röhm, SA Chief of Staff, who was killed in the Night of the Long Knives of 30 June 1934. The plot to eliminate Röhm was masterfully executed.**

Left: **Berlin's police force parade their swastika banner in the Lustgarten in 1935.**
Right: **Hitler in a planning session in 1935 with his deputy, Rudolf Hess, on his right. Also present are von Epp, Sauckel and Funk.**

HAUS ELEPHANT
Koch

Left: **Hitler guarded by the SS enters the Reichstag to deliver a speech in February 1938.**
Above: **Hitler, with Sepp Dietrich behind him, salutes the Leibstandarte, his personal guard, after its formation in 1935.**

the Junkers and the *Reichswehr*. On 28 February 1934 Hitler deemed it politic to issue a warning to the SA and also make his position clear *vis à vis* the *Reichswehr*: "the revolution was finished and the only people entitled to bear arms were the *Reichswehr*." However instead of calming down the situation, Hitler's declaration only irritated the SA to such an extent that the *Reichswehr* became restless. Tensions culminated in June 1934 and at the end of that month Hitler decided to solve the SA problem once and for all: the Night of Long Knives took place.

It was the SA who always dreamt of using their long knives on their petty opponents, the bourgeoisie, Junkers and officers. As it turned out it was their party comrades, the SS, who put their knives to good use on them. In June 1934 rumors of another revolution reached such a pitch that the Vice-Chancellor, Franz von Papen, decided to make a public declaration on the subject. While Hitler was on a lightning visit to Mussolini in Venice, Papen addressed the University at Marburg in a speech in which he claimed that there would be no more revolution and henceforth the Christian principles would be applied in national life. This open call excited the SA no end, but also disquieted the dying President and the Army. On his return from Italy Hitler went directly to Neudeck where the President was in residence, ostensibly to report on his foreign visit but really to calm the President and the Army. Blomberg, who was also at Neudeck, told Hitler that the Army "would restore order if necessary." However Hitler now decided to take the matter into his own hands.

It was at this time that Reichsführer SS, Heinrich Himmler, (who was an unknown in politics) told Hitler that Röhm was plotting his downfall and offered Hitler the SS to liquidate the plot. Whether Hitler believed him is immaterial, but since he had to solve the SA problem, he gratefully accepted Himmler's offer. The rumor of the Röhm plot was skillfully released; the Army also knew about it. On 25 June General Werner von Fritsch, the Army's Commander-in-Chief, put his troops on alert to prevent the SA from seizing power, but Hitler already had matters well in hand. All the actors in this bloody drama were affecting innocence and Röhm agreed to meet Hitler at Bad Wiessee on 30 June 1934; in the meantime he sent his SA troopers on a vacation. Hitler gave plenary powers to Goering and Himmler who, aided by Reinhard Heydrich, drew up the lists of people to be liquidated in the coming purge, for at the last moment Hitler decided not only to square his accounts with the SA, but also to avenge himself on all the other opponents from the past: the conspiracy was enlarged and included even foreign powers (France). On 29 June General von Blomberg stated in the *Völkischer Beobachter* that the Army was behind Hitler, as if to reassure him. At the same time Goebbels confirmed the conspiracy by accusing the Berlin SA leader, Ernst, of planning a *putsch*. On 30 June the purge was launched.

On that day Hitler, accompanied by Victor Lutze, the SA Hanover leader, who was earmarked to take over from Röhm, and by Dietrich, his press spokesman, left by plane for Munich. In Munich, where the *putsch* was supposed to take place, the SA did march in the streets on the previous evening, invited to do so by forged handbills. The SA leaders were

Far left: **Hitler and Hess review a parade of the Leibstandarte Adolf Hitler in Weimar in 1936.**
Left: **The Leibstandarte Adolf Hitler goosesteps past Hitler on his birthday, 20 April 1938.**

somewhat confused, but ultimately managed to get the troopers off the streets. On landing in Munich Hitler ordered the arrest of the SA Munich leader, Schneidhuber, and he himself rushed off to Bad Wiessee, where the top SA leaders were waiting for him. As they arrived Hitler's SS bodyguard found the SA leaders, who were all homosexuals, installed in a comfortable hotel, sleeping, some of them with their male companions. The SS shot Edmund Heines dead on the spot, arrested the rest and drove them off to prison in Munich. On that day some 150 leaders were arrested and summarily executed; SS execution squads were kept busy throughout the three days of the weekend. Röhm refused to commit suicide and was executed by two SS men. Three *Obergruppenführer*s, Heines, von Krausser and Schneidhuber, died executed as did the SA leaders from Saxony and Pomerania, Hayn and von Haydebreck; Ernst of Berlin was taken off a boat at Bremen before he had time to leave for his honeymoon and was executed in Berlin semi-conscious and with a *Heil Hitler* on his lips. However Hitler seems to have made use of this opportunity to rid himself of anyone who had annoyed him in the past: General von Schleicher and his wife, General von Bredow and Gregor Strasser who allegedly were the pivots of the Röhm conspiracy. Vice-Chancellor von Papen had his office wrecked; two of his staff, Edgar Jung the author of his Marburg speech and Herbert

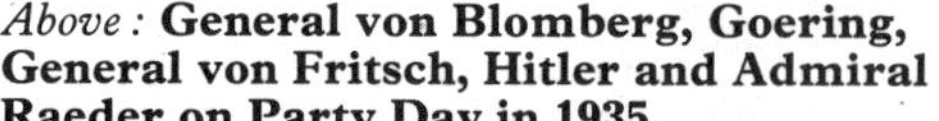

Above: **General von Blomberg, Goering, General von Fritsch, Hitler and Admiral Raeder on Party Day in 1935.**

not want to commit herself. Still this ambivalence was later exploited by the USSR.

On 22 September, after he had obtained Czech capitulation, Chamberlain arrived at Bad Godesberg for another meeting with Hitler. He now offered Hitler his own solution of the Sudeten problem and was shocked to learn that Hitler had in the meantime changed his mind. He now wanted the Sudetenland occupied by the German Wehrmacht by 28 September 1938. The appeasers both in France and Britain surely should have their eyes opened: both the British and French Cabinets rejected these new demands and on 24 September France ordered partial mobilization. Quite unperturbed Hitler delivered his violent speech abusing President Beneš openly at the Sportpalast, Berlin and the following day gave Sir Horace Wilson, who came to Berlin to offer the supervision of the transfer of Sudeten Germans, an ultimatum: if the Czechs did not agree to the German occupation of the Sudetenland, Germany would be at war with Britain and France. Under this threat the appeasers panicked and capitulated.

Above: **Hitler discusses the technical problems of the occupation of the Sudetenland at Munich with his General Staff, from the left Generals Keitel, von Stülpnagel and Blaskowitz.**

Hitler sent Chamberlain another letter in which he defended his attitude to the Czechs and which left it to Chamberlain to mediate. The danger of war was apparently so great that Chamberlain offered Hitler a Four-Power Conference which would resolve the Czech crisis without war. Chamberlain wired Mussolini to sponsor this conference which the Italian dictator convoked at Munich. On 28 September, the date when Hitler's ultimatum expired, the French offered Hitler the surrender of a greater part of the Sudetenland without even consulting the Czechs. They also agreed to participate at the Four-Power Conference, well prepared to give in to Hitler: the only people who were not asked to attend were the representatives of Czechoslovakia itself. The Munich Conference lasted only two days, between 29–30 September, and as a result Hitler got even more than he had asked for at Bad Godesberg. For a paper concession never to go to war against France or Britain, he received not only the entire Sudetenland, but also the mixed regions, all without a plebiscite. Czechoslovakia lost not only its fortifications but also had its transport system, roads and railways, as well as telephone and telegraph disrupted. Premiers Chamberlain and Daladier thought that by means of these terrible concessions they had saved world peace and the rest of Czechoslovakia. However as soon as the conference was over Hitler told General Keitel that he would smash Czechoslovakia – meaning the pitiful remnants – despite the Munich *Diktat*: he was quite bent on a war.

Hitler was determined to bring to the logical conclusion the two projects that he set out to accomplish: swallow up the whole of Czechoslovakia and annex Danzig. In the former case he now thought that he could complete the operation by encouraging autonomist forces without a war. His first step in this direction was an agreement with France guaranteeing her existing frontiers. When, however, the Czechoslovak Foreign Minister asked for a similar guarantee, despite promises in Munich, it was not forthcoming. Instead Hitler began to think of further penetration east by means of independent Slovakia and Goering invited Slovak leaders to Berlin with this in view. Although the remnant of Czechoslovakia was in many ways "simplified" as the Nazis demanded in Munich, the country still continued more or less to function in a liberal democratic fashion. However with the increasing Nazi pressure and encouragement, President Emil Hácha, in order to avoid the break-up of the country, suspended autonomous arrangements and proclaimed emergency laws. Internally Czechoslovakia was on a brink of disaster and Hitler decided to accelerate the process. Then on 11 March 1939 Hitler became convinced that he could destroy the country with bluffing: when Monsignor Josef Tiso, the Slovak leader, arrived in Berlin, he was told to either proclaim independence or be occupied by the Wehrmacht. On 13 March Tiso proclaimed Slovakia independent. Next President Hácha was called to Berlin and after being subjected to unprecedented threats and blackmail he collapsed and signed an invitation to the Wehrmacht to occupy his country. In fact the Wehrmacht occupied part of Moravia even before Hácha's signature on the "invitation" and in any case at 0600 hours, two hours after the signature, on 15 March 1939 the Wehrmacht marched into Czechoslovakia and finally occupied the unfortunate country. Curiously Hitler's partners from Munich, who presided over Czechoslovakia's first dismemberment, failed even to speak out, albeit the French Ambassador did protest in Berlin. Formal notes went out three days later; however by this time both the British and French leaders were finally convinced that no international business could be transacted with Hitler. As if to drive this point home absolutely clearly the Wehrmacht also marched into the city of Memel which it seized from Lithuania.

Thus by the end of March 1939 the Western Allies were forced into protective actions and since the Danzig problem was unresolved Hitler's next move was obvious. In October 1938 the Poles rejected German proposals to resolve the problem "peacefully": Hitler asked the Poles to permit the free city of Danzig to revert to Germany and grant Danzig citizens extraterritorial rights in the Polish corridor separating the city from the Reich. Poland was also to join the Anti-Comintern Pact. In fact the Poles could see that although the Germans offered them peaceful solutions and participation in their expansion in the East, particularly in Lithuania, a country in which the Poles had historical interests, they were however clearly the next victim of this very same eastward expansion. When in February 1939 the Polish Foreign Minister Beck visited London and Paris he was very pessimistic and sounded alarm about German intentions. The Western Allies had their worst fears confirmed by the events in Czechoslovakia, but still did not feel strong enough to offer the Poles diplomatic and military support on their own: they wanted to have the USSR on their side and initiated talks with the USSR with this in view. The Poles felt most uncomfortable: on the one hand they were under pressure from Germany to join the Anti-Comintern Pact and have their security guaranteed. On the other hand the Western Allies offered them a similar guarantee with the USSR, whom they considered as dangerous to their security as Germany. On 31 March 1939, because of Polish opposition, Britain and France jointly undertook to guarantee the Polish frontiers leaving the USSR out of it and three days later Hitler issued the top secret directive *Fall Weiss*, signifying the invasion and destruction of Poland.

Above: **Martin Bormann (left) and Hitler greet Dr Neumann, who helped undermine the Lithuanian government's hold on Memel. Memel was taken on 22 March 1939 shortly before this photograph was taken.**

However before this could be implemented the two real antagonists,the Western Allies and Germany, had to sort out the problem of Soviet Russia. Britain and France, despite the Polish reluctance, continued their talks with the Soviets and in the teeth of Stalin's speech in March 1939, in which he criticized the Western Allies rather severely. On 28 April 1939 Hitler renounced his Non-Aggression Pact with Poland and in the same breath failed to criticize "Bolshevism" and the USSR. It was obvious that the two antagonists were both courting the USSR which was the last obstacle to an open conflict and a decisive factor in the balance of power. Both antagonists tried to tidy up their grouping: Germany reached an economic agreement with Rumania without whose oil it could not wage a war. Next Franco's Spain joined the Anti-Comintern Pact. Germany maintained good relations with Hungary, Bulgaria and Yugoslavia while it signed defense pacts with Latvia, Lithuania and Estonia. The Pact of Steel with Italy followed after Mussolini had annexed Albania. The Western Allies also signed guarantees and agreements: in April with Greece and Rumania, while President Roosevelt appealed to Hitler personally not to go to war. Still all hinged on the USSR.

In May 1939, when Foreign Minister Maxim Litvinov was replaced by Vlachislav Molotov, the Western Allies could see that they were losing out. This did not

Above : **Prime Minister Neville Chamberlain waves the Munich Agreement triumphantly at Heston.**
Left : **The Munich Agreement.**

The Munich Agreement, 29 September 1938

Germany, the United Kingdom, France and Italy, taking into consideration the agreement, which has been already reached in principle for the cession to Germany of the Sudeten German territory, have agreed on the following terms and conditions governing the said cession and the measures consequent thereon, and by this agreement they each hold themselves responsible for the steps necessary to secure its fulfilment:

1 The evacuation will begin on 1 October.

2 The United Kingdom, France and Italy agree that the evacuation of the territory shall be completed by 10 October, without any existing installations having been destroyed and that the Czechoslovak Government will be held responsible for carrying out the evacuation without damage to the said installations.

3 The conditions governing the evacuation will be laid down in detail by an international commission composed of representatives of Germany, the United Kingdom, France, Italy and Czechoslovakia.

4 The occupation by stages of the predominantly German territory by German troops will begin on 1 October. The four territories marked on the attached map will be occupied by German troops in the following order: the territory marked No 1 on 1 and 2 October, the territory marked No II on 2 and 3 October, the territory marked No III on 3, 4 and 5 October, the territory marked No IV on 6 and 7 October. The remaining territory of preponderantly German character will be ascertained by the aforesaid international commission forthwith and be occupied by German troops by 10 October.

5 The international commission referred to in paragraph 3 will determine the territories in which a plebiscite is to be held. These territories will be occupied by international bodies until the plebiscite has been completed. The same commission will fix the conditions in which the plebiscite is to be held, taking as a basis the conditions of the Saar plebiscite. The commission will also fix a date, not later than the end of November, on which the plebiscite will be held.

6 The final determination of the frontiers will be carried out by the international commission. This commission will also be entitled to recommend to the four Powers, Germany, the United Kingdom, France and Italy, in certain exceptional cases minor modifications in the strictly ethnographical determination of the zones which are to be transferred without plebiscite.

7 There will be a right of option into and out of the transferred territories, the option to be exercised within six months from the date of this agreement. A German-Czechoslovak commission shall determine the details of the option, consider ways of facilitating the transfer of population and settle questions of principle arising out of the said transfer.

8 The Czechoslovak Government will within a period of four weeks from the date of this agreement release from their military and police forces any Sudeten Germans who may wish to be released, and the Czechoslovak Government will within the same period release Sudeten German prisoners who are serving terms of imprisonment for political offences.

Munich, 29 September 1938.

ADOLF HITLER
NEVILLE CHAMBERLAIN
EDOUARD DALADIER
BENITO MUSSOLINI

Extract from *Further Documents Respecting Czechoslovakia*. Misc. No. 8 (1938) Cmd. 5848 (HMSO, London, 1938)

prevent them from trying again in July 1939 when they decided to have military talks with the USSR. These seemed the last chance to avert war, for the Western Allies now knew that throughout June 1939 the OKW (*Oberkommando der Wehrmacht*) had been planning war in the East. However these last-chance negotiations went off slowly and proceeded with great difficulties. It was realized subsequently that the Soviets were negotiating with both antagonists, hence the awkwardness. While the talks with the West dragged on, there were swift developments in negotiations with Germany. On 14 August Ribbentrop sent a long message to Molotov outlining the new Non-Aggression Pact and eight days later he flew to Moscow to sign the pact with Stalin. Britain responded with an Alliance Treaty with Poland, but by now neither Poland nor peace could be saved. Hitler had mobilized and even set a date for the attack on Poland and would accept nothing less than a complete surrender by the Poles who were also threatened from the East. Premier Chamberlain had sent Hitler a letter making Britain's position clear in case of an attack on Poland, but Hitler was beyond caring. He made his "last peaceful" effort offering to guarantee the British Empire if Britain kept out of the conflict in Eastern Europe.

While Hitler still claimed that Danzig and Polish atrocities were his reason for attacking Poland he had to stage the Gleiwitz incident to declare war on Poland. This done, on 1 September 1939, the Wehrmacht launched its *blitzkrieg* against Poland. The Western Powers offered paper threats to the invader, but when these failed Britain and France felt obliged to declare war on Germany. On 3 September 1939 Hitler suffered his first real defeat in international politics when he lost the peace. At this stage he was convinced that in fact war meant his victory, and he abandoned foreign affairs for war affairs which proved even less successful.

TOTAL WAR

BLITZKRIEG IN THE WEST

Paradoxically Hitler's war against the West started in the East with the lightning campaign (Blitzkrieg) against Poland. As has been demonstrated it was politically well prepared: Germany had a case against Poland in the form of the city of Danzig, Poland's allies were far away and could not intervene decisively and in the East, Germany obtained the USSR's neutrality at the time Hitler issued the Army with the order to march against Poland. The campaign was meticulously prepared. Curiously Hitler gave the Army a free hand – for the first and last time.

The Polish border with Germany stretched over some 3500 miles and at the best of times would have been difficult to defend; with the Danzig corridor splitting Poland, it was impossible. Moreover, because of the corridor, the Polish Army was under a constant threat of double encirclement. Field Marshal Rydz-Smigly decided to ignore these basic factors of Poland's defense, and concentrate on the defense of the industrial border areas. In July 1939 over a million Poles were mobilized and armies were disposed accordingly, in the proximity of the border. They consisted of some thirty infantry divisions of the Regular Army, while the Reserves, consisting of eleven cavalry brigades, were not yet properly organized. The Polish Army had some 500 obsolete aircraft and for its mobility it had to rely on the railways, which was its chief weakness. Army equipment also proved obsolete and given the basic foot mobility the Polish Army could not hope to defend itself in the modern way: it could not withdraw, nor bring up its reserves; neither could it re-group nor counterattack. All it could do was to stay put and fight to the death – and this it did in several instances – or to fragment under the impact of German attack, get enveloped and surrender, which was its actual fate. However even then the Germans did not have it all their own way; although they tried hard to seize the Dirschau bridge over the Vistula, the Poles succeeded in blowing it up in the last moment.

Below: **SA Chief of Staff Victor Lutze addresses his men at the outbreak of the war. By 1936 the SA's military role in the Third Reich had lapsed. It remained as an ineffective counter to the SS.**

Hitler ordered the OKW to prepare *Fall Weiss* long before the actual attack and on 25 March 1939 warned the soldiers most solemnly, fixing the attack for 26 August 1939. Still it appears that Hitler quite unreasonably expected to avoid a large-scale war, especially after he had succeeded in procuring Soviet neutrality. The Wehrmacht prepared to launch the attack with some 59 divisions, fourteen of which were mechanized, supported by some 1600 Luftwaffe aircraft. The armies were grouped in the north under General Fedor von Bock (Third Army under General Georg Küchler and Fourth under General Günther von Kluge) and in the south under General Gerd von Rundstedt (with the Eighth Army commanded by General Johannes von Blaskowitz and the Fourteenth by General Wilhelm von List). The Tenth Army under General Walther von Reichenau occupied a western position in between the Army groups and was to strike directly against Warsaw. The tactical plan envisaged the Fourth Army striking from Pomerania into the Polish corridor, while the Third Army struck at the corridor from East Prussia. Then the two armies would combine in their drive on Warsaw. In the south the Eighth and Fourteenth Armies were striking north-east from Silesia and Slovakia to meet with all the other armies outside Warsaw. German superiority in men and equipment was so clear that Poland's Allies thought that Germany would be overwhelmingly successful; still no one expected that the German Blitzkrieg would only take three weeks to accomplish the destruction of Poland.

On the eve of the invasion Hitler told

Above: **Generals Paulus, von Brauchitsch and Keitel go over the map of eastern Poland during the month-long Polish campaign of September 1939.**
Right: **The Molotov-Ribbentrop Pact of August 1939.**

The Non-Aggression Pact between Germany and the USSR, 23 August 1939

Guided by the desire to strengthen the cause of peace between Germany and the Union of Socialist Soviet Republics, and basing themselves on the fundamental stipulations of the Neutrality Agreement concluded between Germany and the Union of Socialist Soviet Republics in April, 1926, the German Government and the Government of the Union of Socialist Soviet Republics have come to the following agreement.

Article 1 The two contracting parties undertake to refrain from any act of force, any aggressive act, and any attacks against each other undertaken either singly or in conjunction with any other Powers.

Article 2 If one of the contracting parties should become the object of war-like action on the part of a third Power, the other contracting party will in no way support the third Power.

Article 3 The Governments of the two contracting parties will in future remain in consultation with one another in order to inform each other about questions which touch their common interests.

Article 4 Neither of the two contracting parties will join any group of Powers which is directed, mediately or immediately, against the other party.

Article 5 In case disputes or conflicts on questions of any kind should arise between the two contracting parties, the two partners will solve these disputes or conflicts exclusively by friendly exchange of views or if necessary by arbitration commissions.

Article 6 The present agreement is concluded for the duration of ten years with the stipulation that unless one of the contracting partners denounces it one year before its expiration, it will automatically be prolonged by five years.

Article 7 The present agreement shall be retified in the shortest possible time. The instruments of ratification are to be exchanged in Berlin. The treaty comes into force immediately it has been signed.

Done in two original documents in the German and Russian languages, respectively.

MOSCOW, 23 August, 1939. For the German Government RIBBENTROP

As plenipotentiary of the Government of the Union of Socialist Soviet Republics MOLOTOV

Extract from German Library of Information's *Documents on the Events Preceding The Outbreak of the War* New York, 1940)

his generals about a new type of warfare in which he was engaging: the war objective was not only the destruction of the Polish Armies but the destruction of the Polish nation, a task which would be accomplished by handpicked SS troops (*Einsatztruppen*) who would be operating alongside the advancing armies. He did not specify these special task duties, but all the assembled generals guessed what Hitler was talking about; they all felt uneasy, for this type of warfare was indeed an innovation. None, however, felt strong enough to refuse permission to the SS troops to operate in their military zones. Neither did any one of them resign in protest as they were all totally absorbed with the execution of the invasion.

On 1 September 1939 the German Armies and Luftwaffe attacked Poland and the latter destroyed Polish aircraft on the ground and completely disrupted the railways. In the south there was some

Right: **Hitler flanked by Martin Bormann and Gauleiter Forster on the Long Bridge in Danzig after the city was taken on the first day of World War II.**

Left: **Junkers Ju 52 transport over Poland.**
Right: **A squadron of Stukas which were assigned to bombing airfields behind the Polish lines. Stukas also pounded key road and rail points, which threw the retreating Polish Army into confusion.**

Directive No 1 for the Conduct of the War

1 Since the situation on Germany's Eastern frontier has become intolerable and all political possibilities of peaceful settlement have been exhausted, I have decided upon a *solution by force.*

2 The attack on Poland will be undertaken in accordance with the preparations made for 'Case White,' with such variations as may be necessitated by the build up of the Army which is now virtually complete.

The allocation of tanks and the purpose of the operation remain unchanged.

Date of attack 1 September 1939.

This time also applies to operations at Gdynia, in the Bay of Danzig, and at the Dirschau bridge.

3 In the *West* it is important to leave the responsibility for opening hostilities unmistakably to England and France. Minor violations of the frontier will be dealt with, for the time being, purely as local incidents.

The assurances of neutrality given by us to Holland, Belgium, Luxembourg, and Switzerland are to be meticulously observed.

The Western frontier of Germany will not be crossed *by land* at any point without my explicit orders.

This applies also to all acts of warfare *at sea* or to acts which might be regarded as such.

The defensive activity of the *Air Force* will be *restricted* for the time being to the firm repulse of enemy air attacks on the frontiers of the Reich. In taking action against individual aircraft or small formations, care will be taken to respect the frontiers of neutral countries as far as possible. Only if considerable forces of French or British bombers are employed against German territory across neutral areas will the Air Force be permitted to go into defensive action over neutral soil.

It is particularly important that any infringement of the neutrality of other states by our Western enemies be immediately reported to the High Command of the Armed Forces.

4 Should England and France open hostilities against Germany, it will be the duty of the Armed Forces operating in the West, while conserving their strength as much as possible, to maintain conditions for the successful conclusion of operations against Poland. Within these limits enemy forces and war potential will be damaged as much as possible. The right to order *offensive* operations is reserved absolutely to me.

The *Army* will occupy the West Wall and will take steps to secure it from being outflanked in the north, through the violation by the Western powers of Belgian or Dutch territory. Should French forces invade Luxembourg the bridges on the frontier may be blown up.

The *Navy* will operate against merchant shipping, with England as the focal point. In order to increase the effect, the declaration of danger zones may be expected. The Naval High Command will report on the areas which it is desirable to classify as danger zones and on their extent. The text of a public declaration in this matter is to be drawn up in collaboration with the Foreign Office and to be submitted to me for approval through the High Command of the Armed Forces.

The Baltic Sea is to be secured against enemy intrusion. Commander in Chief Navy will decide whether the entrances to the Baltic should be mined for this purpose.

The *Air Force* is, first of all, to prevent action by the French and English Air Forces against the Germany Army and German territory.

In operations against England the task of the Air Force is to take measures to dislocate English imports, the armaments industry, and the transport of troops to France. Any favorable opportunity of an effective attack on concentrated units of the English Navy, particularly on battleships or aircraft carriers, will be exploited. The decision regarding attacks on London is reserved to me.

Attacks on the English homeland are to be prepared, bearing in mind that inconclusive results with insufficient forces are to be avoided in all circumstances.

Signed: ADOLF HITLER

Extract from H R Trevor-Roper *Hitler's War Directives, 1939-1945* (London, 1964). Quoted by permission of Sidgwick & Jackson Limited.

stubborn fighting, but by 4 September the German Armies had broken through the Polish lines and began to roll and march on Warsaw, often by-passing large pockets of Polish forces. In the south some six or seven Polish divisions succeeded in withdrawing but were caught up and encircled south of Warsaw in the second week of the campaign. In the northwest large undefeated Polish forces attempted a breakthrough to Warsaw, but were encircled and surrendered. General Heinz Guderian's Panzers struck out of East Prussia, east of Warsaw taking Brest-Litovsk on 17 September; in the south Lvov held out until 21 September. Hitler wanted to take Warsaw before his Soviet ally, who now expressed its desire to join in rather than remain neutral, could launch attacks against the hapless Poles from the east. The city was subjected to intensive air and artillery bombardment and after 56 hours of resistance the Polish Army surrendered. On 17 September the Soviet armies joined the war and a week later Hitler and Stalin divided Poland between themselves even before actual fighting ceased. Hitler controlled the provinces of Warsaw and Lub-

Left: **Hitler's First Directive at the outbreak of fighting in 1939.**
Below: **Hermann Goering observes aircraft on a Polish airfield used to bomb Warsaw in late September 1939.**

Above: **Hitler driven by his aide Kempka with General Keitel and another aide Schmundt in the rear somewhere near the fighting outside Warsaw.**

lin right up to the river Bug while Stalin swallowed up the Polish east including Lithuania. Before all resistance stopped on 5 October Poland, divided between its two neighbors, ceased to exist as a state; its government, administration and part of its armed forces withdrew from the country and through Rumania and Hungary found refuge in France. In the meantime the Soviets and Germans took over the administration of the defeated Poland.

Below: **Axmann, General von Falkenhorst and Vidkun Quisling, whose name has been synonymous with treason since 1940.**

The stories of atrocities during the campaign were confirmed by eye witnesses, among them the American journalist, William Shirer, but this was only a beginning. Even the most appalling massacre of some 50 Jews by SS artillery men paled into insignificance after the arrival of Reinhard Heydrich, Himmler's deputy, to execute Hitler's ideas of genocide. On 21 September 1939 Heydrich produced his plan for the "housecleaning of Jews, intelligentsia, clergy and the nobility in Poland," which again appalled the Army, but which was nevertheless carried out by the newly appointed Governor General of the remnants of the Polish state. Within a year over 1,200,000 Poles were deported from the newly annexed German provinces eastward, while Governor Hans Frank boasted of summary sentences on two batches of Polish intellectuals, some 2500 and 3500 each. Hitler's Germany demonstrated in the case of Poland, how it would launch wars, carry them out and what consequences it would have in store for the defeated country.

In the meantime, while all this was going on in Poland, Hitler made his "last effort" to re-establish peace. On 7 October 1939 in a speech in the Reichstag Hitler offered a comprehensive peace settlement to France and Britain, which was turned down, for the Western Allies by now fully realized what the *pax germanica* had meant in Poland. Hitler, therefore, turned his mind to the conquest in the West. The Polish campaign which he left almost entirely to his generals to plan and execute, nevertheless confirmed him in his opinion that he possessed extraordinary strategic and tactical instincts, and he now proceeded with the planning of the war in the West. On 9 October 1939 he issued a memorandum justifying his policies and at the same time issued directives for the *Fall Gelb*, the conquest of France and Britain via Holland and Belgium. While he wanted to "start this war to end the war" as soon as possible it had to be postponed again and again, for the weather and the Western Allies offered him important distractions which he could not ignore.

While the Eastern Campaign secured him oil supplies in Rumania and the Soviet Union, it also exposed his only supply of iron ore from Sweden to new dangers. For, while the "Phony War" on land continued unabated, real war was being waged at sea. As early as 3 September the *U.30* sank the liner *Athenia* with the loss of 112 lives, many of them American. British merchant shipping losses amounted to ten per week. Moreover the aircraft carrier, *Courageous*, was sunk by *U.29*, while the battleship *Royal Oak* sunk at anchor at Scapa Flow. However Admiral Raeder only had a small naval force at his disposal and soon the British fleet began to assert itself in the North Sea. For two months it chased the two German pocket battleships to no avail, but it did prove to Hitler that it could cut his vital shipping line from Sweden via Narvik. Then the Soviet–Finnish war broke out, and it made Scandinavian public opinion not only sharply anti-Soviet, but also anti-German. Hitler began to fear that the Swedes might terminate iron ore deliveries, especially if the Norwegians decided to loan Narvik as a supply base to the Western Allies for their aid to Finland. On 14 December 1939, in this atmosphere of tensions, the

Norwegian fascist leader, Quisling, met Hitler and invited him to make sure of Norway by occupying it. Though Hitler seemed busy with the preparations for war in the West, he immediately ordered the *Oberkommando der Wehrmacht* (OKW) to investigate this possibility, but what finally decided him to have another dress rehearsal campaign before attacking France was the incident with the *Altmark*, which Allied warships cornered in a Norwegian fjord relieving it of its cargo of Allied POWs. In February 1940 he told General Falkenhorst exactly what he wanted in Norway and ordered him to plan and subsequently command the expedition.

Albeit the reasons for the occupation of Denmark and Norway were largely economic and naval; Hitler still wanted to confirm the efficacy of his blitzkrieg tactics in these more difficult conditions than in Poland. Once again surprise, speed and concentration were to achieve victory. Integration of all arms was indispensable and the command itself had to be restructured so that more initiative could be left to those lower down executing the general plan. This made leadership on all levels more dynamic; excellent communications and co-ordination were essential. In these conditions Hitler determined what tasks the Armed Forces were to perform and when, and victory seemed assured both in Scandinavia and France. The Allies in fact hesitated so long that Hitler set operations in motion a day before the Allies started to mine the seas off Norway in order to threaten Germany's supply line. On 7 April 1940 two groups of German warships sailed for Norway.

The operation was perfectly integrated and the Germans achieved their objectives with token forces only. Copenhagen and Denmark were occupied on the way, and the Germans gained advanced airfields as well as sheltered sea corridors for further journeys to Norway. When the forces reached Norway, coastal batteries caused limited damage to German shipping, but their integrated operations were too much for the Norwegians: one parachute bat-

Left: **Wehrmacht troops advance during the Norwegian campaign, in which the Germans ran into stiff opposition.**

talion seized two airfields and henceforth the Luftwaffe's intervention became decisive. There was a bit of fighting at Trondheim and Bergen, but none at Oslo. After the initial resistance to the landing itself, the King and the government had time to slip away into exile. Only after 14 April did British and French troops begin to arrive. First of all they tried to recapture Trondheim, but were beaten off, because they lacked air support. Allied intervention north of Oslo proved equally indecisive and after a week of confused fighting the troops were withdrawn. The face-saving operation against Narvik soon ran into difficulty. The tiny German garrison was only dislodged on 27 May, when France was on the point of collapse. Ten days later

Right: **Trucks are unloaded on a Norwegian dock to support the German invasion.**

the troops were ordered out of Norway having only achieved the destruction of the port of Narvik and its ore-handling installations. However before this diversionary blitzkrieg came to an end, Hitler had launched his drive against France and Britain.

In the West it was obvious that operations could not be launched before the winter was out; nevertheless Hitler fixed a firm date for 17 January 1940. Fortunately for the Allies, German plans of this attack fell into their hands a week before its execution; still the weather postponed operations. By then the Allies knew that the attack would be delivered from the Netherlands and they evolved Plan D which meant that they would move into Belgium.

Below: **Wehrmacht troops watch a supply ship arrive in a Norwegian fjord.**

Left: **Dutch artillery was of little use against the might of the German Army during the five-day conquest of Holland in May 1940.**
Right: **Dutch citizens watch the burning city of Rotterdam.**
Far right: **German soldiers watch a ship of the Holland–America line steam out of Rotterdam after its occupation.**

Apart from this planning innovation they failed to make use of the respite: their troop movements were slow and disposition of tanks unimaginative. Though they were inferior to the Germans in anti-aircraft and anti-tank weapons, they were superior to them in men (four million to two million), aircraft and tanks. However their strategic concepts were static and defensive, while Hitler was improving his dynamic strategy all the time. Earlier he had accepted General Manstein's plan for the annihilation of the enemy north of the river Somme. Then he decided on the main thrust via Sedan and for this purpose transferred practically all the Panzer force from Army Group B (Belgium) to Army Group A (Sedan); 44 divisions, of these seven armored ones, were going to break through and drive to the Channel under General von Rundstedt.

On 10 May 1940 Hitler finally launched his operations in the West. On that day Ribbentrop summoned the Belgian and Dutch ambassadors to tell them that German troops would invade their respective countries in order to prevent the Western Allies from occupying them. Although the previous night Colonel Sas, the Dutch military attaché in Berlin, had been warned of the impending attacks by General Oster, and passed on the information both to Brussels and The Hague, the invasion, spearheaded by dive bombers, the *Stukas*, created indescribable chaos and panic. Rather belatedly both the Belgian and Dutch governments sent frantic appeals to the French and British Allies for help. However Plan D was ready and the whole of the BEF as well as the bulk of the French Army in the north moved up into Belgium to help the Low Countries. However far from saving these countries the Anglo-French armies walked into a trap. It took the Germans five days to smash the Dutch armies. On 10 May German paratroopers landed near Rotterdam and the Hague capturing bridges and airfields. General Küchler's Eighteenth Army then attacked on a broad front and forced the Dutch Army as well as the French who had rushed up to Breda to fall back. When on 13 May a German armored division effected a junction with the paratroops near Rotterdam, Queen Wilhelmina and her government left the country for England. On 14 May the Germans issued an ultimatum to the Dutch to surrender or they would flatten Dutch cities with their *Stukas*; then, possibly by mistake, they actually did smash the business center of Rotterdam to smithereens causing some 1000 civilian casualties. Late on that day General Winckelman surrendered and the elements of the Eighteenth Army poured down south towards Antwerp to aid General von Reichenau and his Sixth Army. The irony of this most successful military operation was that it was quite unnecessary: it was only included in *Fall Gelb* on the Luftwaffe's request for its future operations against Britain.

It was thought that the Belgian Army, which consisted of some fifteen divisions, would hold up the invading Germans longer than it did. It was not because the Belgians fought badly but Reichenau's troops were magnificently prepared and fought like lions. Specially trained paratroopers were landed beyond Belgian lines and seized the three important bridges before the Belgians guarding them could blow them up. The impregnable Fort Eben

Left: **Wehrmacht anti-aircraft in Holland destroy the few planes which attacked their position near The Hague.**

EENDAM-HOLLAND

Emael with its garrison of 1200 men surrendered after a surprise attack by eighty German paratroopers: they used special explosives to blow holes in its roof and then kept the garrison helpless for thirty hours. These feats of valor as well as the sustained pressure of Reichenau's Sixth Army supported by General Erich Höpner's XVI Panzer Corps forced the Belgians to fall back steadily though more rapidly than was calculated. When the Dutch surrendered no one had the slightest idea that the Belgians would entertain the same idea; after all, under the steady pressure of the invading armies all the Allied Armies were retreating. Then suddenly, out of the blue, the Belgian Army surrendered unconditionally leaving a huge gap in the right wing of the Allied Front.

During the early fighting much confusion was caused by the implementation of Plan D which made General Henri Giraud's 7th Army dash up to Holland and the BEF under Lord Gort to Belgium. Holland's collapse increased the mobility of Allied forces and not much time was left for co-ordination and consultation. The King of the Belgians as Commander-in-Chief of the Belgian Army was tactfully left to his own devices and was told nothing of Allied intentions. He had witnessed the surrender of Holland and heard about the breakthrough in the Ardennes area; on 24 May he heard that Calais had been

Below : **A damaged ship of the Holland–America Line in Rotterdam after the air attack.**
Right : **Luftwaffe paratroops get ready for the aerial assault on Holland the night before the invasion of 10 May 1940.**
Below left : **The nose of a Ju 88 bomber.**

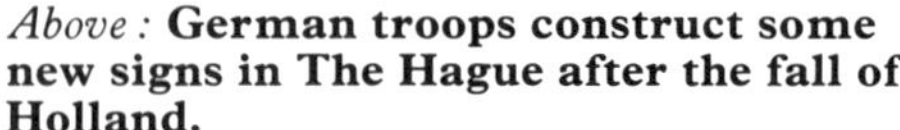
Above : **German troops construct some new signs in The Hague after the fall of Holland.**

Above : **General Kurt Student inspects paratroops before their assault on Fort Eben Emael in Belgium.**
Above right : **Marshal Philippe Pétain, who took over the French government after the debacle in May–June 1940.**
Above far right : **Pierre Laval, Pétain's Premier, meets Hitler after the fall of France.**
Right : **From left to right General Keitel, Hitler, General Jodl and Martin Bormann at the Führer's headquarters on the Western Front in Belgium in June 1940.**

surrounded by German troops and that made him panic. The following day he held a meeting with his government and told them about his intention to sue for peace. The government unanimously rejected the proposal and constitutionally the King should have abdicated or gone into total exile. Instead he dispatched General Derousseaux to the Germans, who brought back Hitler's conditions for a cease-fire. Early in the morning of 28 May hostilities between the Belgian and German Armies ceased, for the King had accepted Hitler's conditions. He thought that the Allied cause was lost and that he had saved Belgium, but was wrong on both counts: the Allies certainly lost the Battle of France, but not the war. As for Belgium itself Leopold's government condemned him and went into exile, while the Belgians had to suffer the indignities of German occupation for the rest of the war.

With the Dutch and Belgian disasters the Anglo-French Allies began to sense that an even greater one was in the offing. As in the case of the German military leaders, the French and British generals had only paid scanty attention to the area round Sedan which was outside the Maginot defensive perimeter and in unsuitable terrain for large-scale offensive actions, especially by tanks. It was precisely for this reason that General von Manstein suggested that the Wehrmacht should concentrate its armor there, break through the hills and then cut across the plains to the Channel splitting Allied defenses in two. While the Wehrmacht in the person of the Chief of Staff, General Franz Halder, disliked this "eccentric" plan, Hitler immediately fell for it, and in time came to believe that it was in fact he who thought of it first. In any case he gave personal orders to concentrate General Hermann Hoth's XV Panzer Corps, General Reinhardt's XLI Panzer Corps and General Guderian's XIX Panzer Corps in this sector. All these Panzer forces, under General Ewald von Kleist's command, would carry out Hitler's "breakthrough plan." It so happened that this devastating attack fell on the weakest elements of the feeble 2nd Army (General Huntziger) and the 9th Army (General Corap); moreover the Generalissimo Gamelin had no strategic reserves in this area and only had cavalry formations to slow down German armor. By nightfall on 11 May Guderian's XIX Panzer Corps was in the vicinity of Sedan and two days later General Rommel's 7th Panzer Division controlled a bridgehead across the Meuse. Although Huntziger counterattacked with cavalry the following day and despite the Royal Air Force bombers bombing the vital bridge, all these efforts failed to halt or even slow down the Germans. Guderian's and Reinhardt's offensive punched a hole some 50 miles wide in the Allied Front. The German invaders were formidable; they used the *Stukas* instead of heavy artillery, but also had self-propelled guns; mechanized infantry followed the armored formations and engineers used rubber boats to cross rivers throwing up pontoon bridges. By 17 May the three armored columns which broke through the French front were halfway to the Channel and for the first time they had to face a serious counterattack. The newly promoted General Charles de Gaulle assembled a newly created armored division north of Laôn and advanced against the southern flank of the armored thrust. Since de Gaulle remained unsupported he soon had to break off the engagement, and the German armor could pour on.

Curiously and certainly not as a result of de Gaulle's counterattack, Hitler himself lost his nerve, and ordered the armor to halt. Both he and Rundstedt who was in overall command of this Army Group expected a massive French counterattack with the aim of cutting through the thin line of German armor. For two days Hitler held up his armored force, albeit their advance really continued under the guise of a "reconnaissance in force." What probably confused the Führer was General Maurice Gamelin's plan of an offensive from both north and south to prevent the Germans splitting the front into two. However on 19 May General Gamelin was relieved of command and his

Right: **A turret of the Maginot Line, which proved no adequate defense for France. It was outflanked.**
Far right: **The triumphal parade staged by the Nazis after their seizure of Paris on 14 June 1940. They moved up the Avenue Foch, shown here, and down the Champs Elysées.**

successor, General Maxime Weygand, cancelled the combined counteroffensive. On 20 May, when Hitler gave his Armies the green light to roll on again, the 2nd Panzer Division reported that it had reached Abbeville thus cutting the armies in the north from the south. On 21 May Lord Gort and the French 1st Army made a last attempt at breaking south near Arras, but when this last attempt failed, all dissolved in chaos.

Whether the Germans were also affected by the general chaos of the fighting is still unclear and disputed. By 24 May Guderian's tanks had captured Boulogne, bypassed Calais and were within sight of Dunkirk, when they were again halted on Hitler's personal orders. In the north the Belgians were about to surrender, while the French 1st Army was holding a salient southeast of Lille. General Gamelin's orders for re-grouping and counterattack certainly made sense, but they served only to disorganize still further the demoralized French and British troops and command. The newly appointed Commander-in-Chief not only cancelled the counteroffensive, but also failed to restore morale in the north; despite his seeing King Leopold (or perhaps because of it) the Belgians surrendered. General Billotte would probably not have restored French morale in any case after his talk with Weygand; mercifully he was killed in a car accident before he could even start. Weygand did not find Lord Gort, the commander of the BEF, and it is not clear whether Gort would have obeyed French orders anyway. As it was he was ordered by Premier Churchill to "save" the BEF by evacuating it from the only remaining port, Dunkirk. Thus the combination of Allied chaos and Hitler's momentary hesitation produced the miracle of Dunkirk.

While General Weygand was roving in Northern France in search of his ally, Lord Gort had decided to cut his losses and withdraw to England. He warned London of his intentions a week in advance and when on 25 May he actually gave orders to start evacuation, the Navy had the situa-

Above right: **A German soldier observes a burning village in northern France in June 1940.**
Right: **A wrecked British ship left at Dunkirk after its capture. By the time it was taken almost 350,000 Allied troops had been evacuated.**

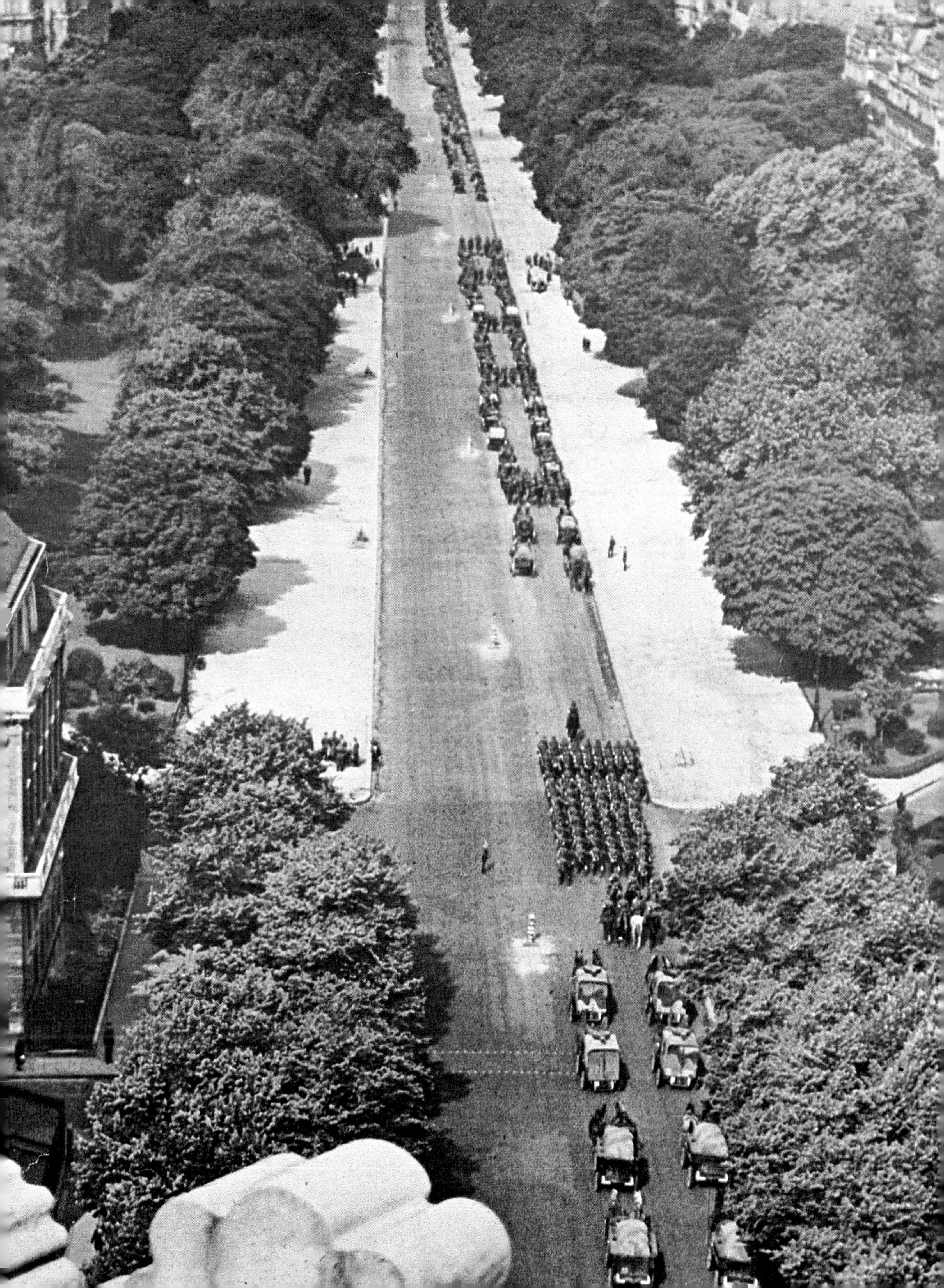

under the command of Field Marshal Wilhelm Ritter von Leeb, struck with its 600 tanks (4th Panzer Group under General Erich Höpner) against the Baltic states and on to Leningrad. In the west, the largest of the armies, Army Group Center, under Field Marshal Fedor von Bock, with two Panzer armies (2nd Panzer Group under General Heinz Guderian and 3rd Panzer Group under General Hermann Hoth) was to deliver the heaviest blow ultimately taking the capital. In the south Field Marshal Gerd von Rundstedt was in command of Army Group South which with its 1st Panzer Group under General, later Field Marshal Ewald von Kleist, was to conquer the Ukraine.

The surprise factor was supreme; while

Above left: **Wehrmacht cavalry pause during the German drive into the USSR in the summer of 1941.**
Above right: **The Wehrmacht during street fighting in Zhitomir, a town in the Ukraine near Kiev which was taken in late summer 1941.**

Left: **A Focke-Wulf 200 Condor bomber, used on both Eastern and Western Fronts during the war.**

Above: **Russian KV tanks begin their encirclement of Stalingrad in the late autumn of 1942, isolating the German Sixth Army.**
Left: **Field Marshal von Kleist wearing his Iron Cross.**

the Soviet Commanders asked Moscow for orders and were at a loss as to what they should do, the German Luftwaffe attacked and destroyed airfields and aircraft thereon, while the army seized important bridges which enabled the Panzers to pour into Russia. Within two days the Russian front was in pieces and the Panzers wheeled round to perform encirclement movements. However the first two cauldrons, *Kessel*, as the Germans called them, were only partially successful. When the Panzers closed the ring around the Bialystok salient the Fourth Army and the Ninth Army were too slow in coming up to destroy the enemy, which largely managed to break through and retreat. From the very beginning, and quite contrary to their experience in the West, the Germans found out that Soviet armies and even leaderless groups of soldiers resisted to the last, thus holding back the infantry which was so necessary for the destruction of the enemy in the massive armor encirclements. Thus the fortress of Brest held out for a week; some 100,000 men of the elite border troops, Soviet security forces, put up hard fights, and even when defeated, tended to carry on fighting as roving partisan bands delaying the progress of German infantry still further. The second cauldron in the Minsk-Bobruysk area also proved unsatisfactory; the infantry was delayed by tough fighting and rain, and most of the trapped enemy managed to escape. Of the planned encirclements only the Smolensk one lived up to the expectations. After hard fighting the Germans captured some 300,000 Russians, among them Stalin's son, but were far from the initial objective of destroying the Soviet Armed Forces. After Smolensk the Panzers of the Center Group were diverted south to help Rundstedt in his encirclement of the

Soviet southwestern armies. Although this proved to be the largest cauldron ever with some 500,000 prisoners taken, it finally dislocated German strategic and tactical plans. Without decisively destroying the Soviet armies the encirclements proved to be much deeper into Russia than was ever envisaged. Operations were hopelessly and irretrievably behind the planned schedule.

It is obvious that Hitler and the German High Command committed a number of mistakes which threw the planned operations badly out of gear. For example, Halder admitted that he underestimated Russian resources: instead of the estimated 200 divisions he found 360 divisions fighting hard despite defeat. The unexpected, suicidal resistance also upset German planning and schedules and was entirely due to the criminal orders which Hitler had issued before the campaign. As their application quickly spread, Russian soldiers preferred to die fighting and by so doing successfully harassed the numerically weak German infantry; even the Panzers began to suffer heavily, becoming technically immobilized, because the Russian partisans refused to surrender. It was quickly noted that Russian resistance was toughest in the operational zones of the 3rd and 4th Panzer Groups, who seem to have applied the *Kommissar* order most consistently. By 8 July these Panzer armies executed 101 and 170 *kommissars* respectively. Soon Soviet soldiers began to retaliate and the German Army became unnerved when it discovered mass evidence of these retaliations.

However the greatest havoc on both sides was caused by the activity of the SS *Einsatzkommandos*: the scale of their operations confirmed the masses of demoralized Russian soldiers in their resistance and retaliation. With typical German bureaucratic thoroughness the *Einsatzgruppen* were organized in four sections. Group A under the command of SS *Brigadeführer* Dr Stahlecker operated in the Baltic states and the Russian North. By 15 October 1941 it succeeded in massacring some 125,000 Jews and 5000 others. Group B under SS Oberführer Dr Naumann operated in the area of Army Group Center and by 14 November reported some 45,000 executions. Group C under the command of Dr Braune and Dr Thomas operated in the Ukraine and in the first three months managed to massacre 75,000 Jews and 5000 others. In the South SS Brigadeführer Dr Ohlendorf operated with his Group D and they *only* liquidated some 55,000 human souls. All the *Einsatzgruppen* operated in military zones and the impact of their activity on both German and Soviet soldiers can be imagined, though not properly evaluated; for example, at Mogilev 337 Jewish women were publicly executed. Moreover other SS groups operated in POW camps and at Borisov they executed 41,752 *kommissars* and 41,357 Jewish POWs. At Borisov also the first 24 Soviet partisans were publicly executed. *Einsatzkommando* 5, which operated deep in the Ukraine, reported 15,110 executions on 20 October, and at the same time the Gestapo became active on the POWs and quickly eliminated them all. On 5 December 1941 Gestapo chief Müller, reported that after screening 22,000 POWs he liquidated 16,000 of them. Altogether 1,030,157 POWs were

Above: **Field Marshal von Kluge issues his orders. Von Kluge was one of Hitler's most competent generals and was known as *Kluger Hans*, Clever John.**

Above: **Russian forces in the trenches surrounding Leningrad at the start of the 900-day siege of the former Czarist capital.**

Right: **Soviet partisans prepare to blow up a railway track behind German lines in the winter of 1942–43.**
Overleaf: **German field artillery is moved up to the front.**

Right: **The T-32 medium tank, a prototype for the famous T-34.**
Far right: **Stalin and Marshal Voroshilov.**
Below: **Soviet boats continue the trickle of supplies across Lake Ladoga which kept Leningrad alive during its long siege.**

liquidated by the SD or shot while trying to escape, which in time proved a more convenient type of execution. At the end of the war only some 1,000,000 POWs survived out of the 5,700,000 captured.

The short-term effect of these atrocities was catastrophic from the German point of view: German soldiers were paralyzed by fear, fought only in close formations refusing to comb large, conquered areas, thus abandoned to the partisans. Long before Hitler and the High Command realized, the common German soldier and his officer felt that they were being trapped in the open spaces of Russia and that they would only come out alive with luck. However their leaders, encouraged by the vast encirclement successes, were determined to drive the Army on, deeper into Russia. On 21 August 1941 Hitler issued an order in which priorities were modified: Moscow was no longer top priority – Hitler, facing opposition from his generals, whom he declared economic ignoramuses, ordered

Above : **Field Marshal von Manstein studies his plan of attack.**
Above right : **German mountain troops engage a distant enemy with their MG42 machine gun.**

Below : **"War Until Victory" was the slogan used on this "Freedom Loan" Soviet poster.**

the conquest of the Crimea, the industrial Donets basin and the cutting off from Russia of the oil supplies in the Caucasus. Although he permitted further attacks on Leningrad, the northern Group soon became stuck and spectacular advances were only noticeable in the south.

It was only in October 1941 that the offensive against Moscow, Operation Typhoon, was resumed. The Panzer formations besieging Leningrad, were transferred to Army Group Center for this offensive, thus saving that city from German occupation. In launching this offensive the German High Command thought that it would end the war. The Germans attacked on a broad front north of Smolensk with Guderian's tanks striking against Bryansk and Hoth's against Vyazma. After a breakthrough they both wheeled round and netted some 500,000 prisoners, thus destroying Stalin's strategic reserves, many brought in from the Far East. Although the infantry again found it difficult to keep up with the tanks, Moscow was unprotected and within easy reach of the armor and infantry. However the Germans began to encounter difficulty they had never even dreamt about: on 7 October the first snow fell and many vehicles broke down as a result. Still they broke through in the northern sector of the front and the town of Kalinin was taken. This provoked panic in Moscow itself and government offices began to be evacuated to Kyubyshev on the Volga. Although defense positions and trenches were being built, the panic affected not only the population but also political leaders who fled from the city. Widespread looting was reported and Stalin, the lonely dictator, who had not panicked, proclaimed martial law in the city and NKVD troops restored order. As for the Germans their advance in the center had been slowed down, while in the south, where Guderian's breakthrough would have sealed Moscow's fate, desperate Russian counterattacks virtually destroyed Guderian's Panzers. Throughout November 1941 the Russians were forced to retreat, sometimes fast, sometimes slowly, but always fighting hard; they harried the advancing Germans using Katyusha mortars against them and even the Red Air Force revived. Still on 12 November the High Command instead of abandoning the offensive because of supply problems, decided to press on despite mud, cold, snow and general exhaustion.

During November 1941 Stalin reorganized the defenses of Moscow. General Georgi Zhukov was appointed Commander to save the capital after all the other generals had failed. Zhukov was reinforced by troops from the Far East and got some 1700 tanks and 1500 aircraft for his counteroffensive, which Stalin approved on 30 November. By now the

LIBERATED BY ALLIES
19 NOVEMBER 1942 – 4 JULY 1943
4 JULY 1943 – 23 JUNE 1944
ALLIED FRONT LINES
2 FEBRUARY 1943
4 JULY 1943
14 JANUARY 1944
23 JUNE 1944
0 MILES 500
0 KILOMETERS 800
ARCTIC OCEAN
Barents Sea
ATLANTIC OCEAN
NORTH SEA
Baltic Sea
Bay of Biscay
BLACK SEA
Caspian Sea
MEDITERRANEAN SEA
White Sea
ICELAND
REYKJAVIK
NORWAY
SWEDEN
FINLAND
RUSSIA
EIRE
GREAT BRITAIN
DENMARK
GERMANY
POLAND
FRANCE
SPAIN
PORTUGAL
ITALY
YUGOSLAVIA
HUNGARY
RUMANIA
BULGARIA
GREECE
TURKEY
ALBANIA
SWITZ.
SLOVAKIA
E.PRUSSIA
NETH.
BELG.
LUX.
SYRIA (Free Fr)
IRAQ (Br)
IRAN
PALESTINE (Br)
TRANSJORDAN (Br)
SAUDI ARABIA
EGYPT (Br prot.)
LIBYA
TUNISIA (Free Fr)
ALGERIA (Free French)
MOROCCO (Free Fr)
SP.MOR.
GIBRALTAR (Br)
Corsica
Sicily
Crete
Cyprus (Br)
Dodecanese
MALTA
Jan 1943
Leningrad relieved
4-23 July 1943
Battle of Kursk
6 June 1944
D-day: Allied forces land in Normandy
15 Aug 1944
Landings in St Tropez area
22 Jan 1944
Landings at Anzio
27 Jan-18 May 1944
Battles for Cassino
Sept 1943
Landings at Reggio (3rd) and Salerno (9th)
8 Sept 1943
Italy surrenders
10 July 1943
Allied forces land in Sicily
11 May 1943
Axis forces in N. Africa surrender
PETSAMO
MURMANSK
NARVIK
ARCHANGEL
TRONDHEIM
BERGEN
OSLO
STOCKHOLM
HELSINKI
VIIPURI
L.Ladoga
PETROZAVODSK
LENINGRAD
TALLINN
PSKOV
RIGA
MOSCOW
TULA
SMOLENSK
KAUNAS
KONIGSBERG
DANZIG
MINSK
KURSK
VORONEZH
Volga
STALINGRAD
KHARKOV
KIEV
Dnieper
Don
ROSTOV
ZAPOROZHYE
ODESSA
NOVOROSSIISK
GROZNY
SEVASTOPOL
TIFLIS
EDINBURGH
DUBLIN
LIVERPOOL
LONDON
AMSTERDAM
HAMBURG
BERLIN
COPENHAGEN
WARSAW
Vistula
BRUSSELS
COLOGNE
Rhine
CHERBOURG
CAEN
PARIS
PRAGUE
LVOV
Danube
MUNICH
VIENNA
BUDAPEST
BERNE
VICHY
BORDEAUX
MILAN
TURIN
VENICE
MARSEILLES
FLORENCE
BELGRADE
BUCHAREST
SOFIA
ISTANBUL
ANKARA
LISBON
MADRID
ROME
CASSINO
ANZIO
NAPLES
SALERNO
PALERMO
REGGIO
ATHENS
DAMASCUS
JERUSALEM
AMMAN
ORAN
ALGIERS
BÔNE
TUNIS
C.Bon
KASSERINE
MARETH
CASABLANCA
TRIPOLI
SIRTE
EL AGHEILA
BENGHAZI
TOBRUK
ALEXANDRIA
EL ALAMEIN
CAIRO
Suez Canal
Nile

that their counterattacks would not work. On 3 September the 1st Guard Army under General Moskalenko did attack, but after advancing a few hundred meters, was beaten back. Stalin told Zhukov to go on attacking and to throw in these attacks all he had, else the city would fall. Two days later the 1st Guards were beaten off again though they retained a few hundred meters of their gain; the 24th Army which by now was also attacking, was, however, beaten to its starting line.

On that very day the Soviets finally noticed that the Germans began to withdraw forces from the central sector where the city was most threatened, transferring them to the north. Zhukov decided to deploy everything he had, from heavy artillery and rockets to aircraft. General Aleksandr Golovanov's long range bombers were sent out every night to bomb German supply bases and lines. General Aleksandr Novikov arrived as Stalin's special air representative together with the 16th Air Army under General Rudenko. Fighter regiments commanded by Generals Khryukin and Stepanov went into action together. After a week of heavy fighting Zhukov reported to Stalin that his forces could not break through in the northern sector and was in turn asked by Stalin to fly to Moscow and report in person. Hitler seems to have had the same idea and Paulus also had to fly to Vinnitsa headquarters. After their departures offensive probings continued; however the Germans succeeded in launching theirs more effectively.

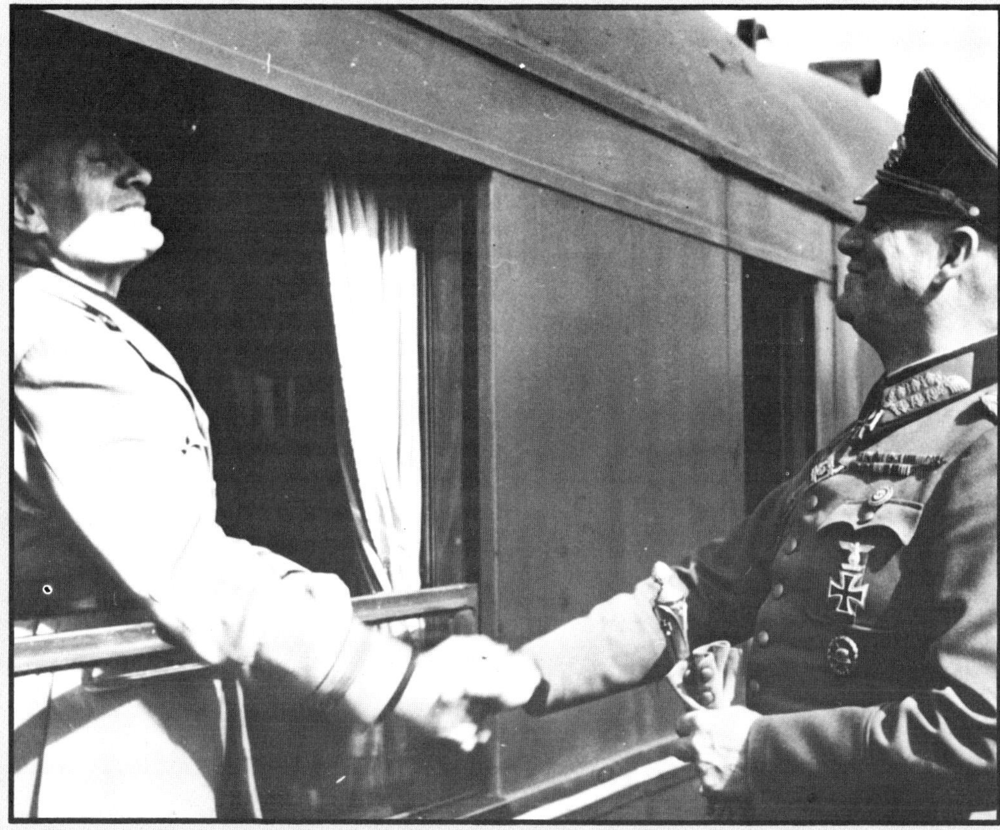

On 12 September the Germans threw into the battle against Stalingrad 11 infantry and three Panzer divisions. Hoth's tanks had broken into the southern suburb, Kuporosnoye, thus dividing the two Russian armies. They also took the Mamaya Kurgan, a height overlooking the city and penetrated into the city itself. All through the night that followed the Russians were ferrying General Rodimtsev's 13th Guards Division across the Volga to stem the German breakthrough. At daybreak the following day, the Germans resumed their two-pronged assault of the city: first, 295th, 71st and 94th Infantry Divisions supported by the XXIV Panzer Corps and second, 20th Motorized Division supported by the XIV Panzer Corps. Although many units and even regiments of the 62nd Army, whose commanding general Lopatin

Above left : **Mussolini says good-bye to Field Marshal Keitel after visiting the Führer in the Wolf's Lair, Hitler's headquarters in East Prussia.**
Above : **A Luftwaffe command post on the Eastern Front.**
Below : **Soviet General Rokossovsky at his command post.**

was sacked the previous day and replaced by Chuikov, were wiped out, it nevertheless contained the breakthrough and held the attack. On 14 September Chuikov tried to stage counterattacks, but his troops could not make much progress after being pinned down by German artillery fire and Stuka bombardment. The fresh 13th Guards, despite aerial bombardment, retook the principal German gains in the central town sector: in hand-to-hand fighting they drove the 71st Division from the main railway station and the 29th Division from the hillock, Mamaya Kurgan.

After this bloody rebuff General Paulus regrouped his forces dividing them into two attacking groups in the center and north. For the center attack he picked the crack 71st Division and the 100th Jäger Division with orders to retake the Mamaya Kurgan, and the station. The bloody fighting continued until 21 September: Mamaya Kurgan was not retaken by the Germans, but the hillock was never covered by snow or anything except shells and fresh earth craters. The station changed hands fifteen times before the 13th Guards consolidated their hold. The diversionary northern attacks were beaten off and Chuikov's counterattacks failed to drive the Germans out of town. This onslaught petered out when both sides became exhausted: but the Germans regrouped and were ready to strike again.

Once again the Russians managed to ferry reinforcements into the city: the fresh Siberian (284th) rifle division with which Chuikov tried a spoiling attack to dislocate German preparations. After a Stuka bombardment on 27 September the Germans resumed their assault, gained over one kilometer of bombed-out ruins, lost some 2000 men and 50 tanks, and came to a standstill exhausted. At night the Russians counterattacked and re-took German gains. By 29 September Paulus committed the regiments of 16th Panzers, 60th Motorized Division and 389th and 100th Infantry Divisions, and switched his efforts to Orlovka where heavy fighting continued.

Above : **Soviet troops advance briskly in the winter of 1942–43.**
Below : **A makeshift German airfield under Soviet aerial attack somewhere west of the Don River in early 1943. Goering's promise of adequate supply lines being maintained to the Sixth Army proved false.**

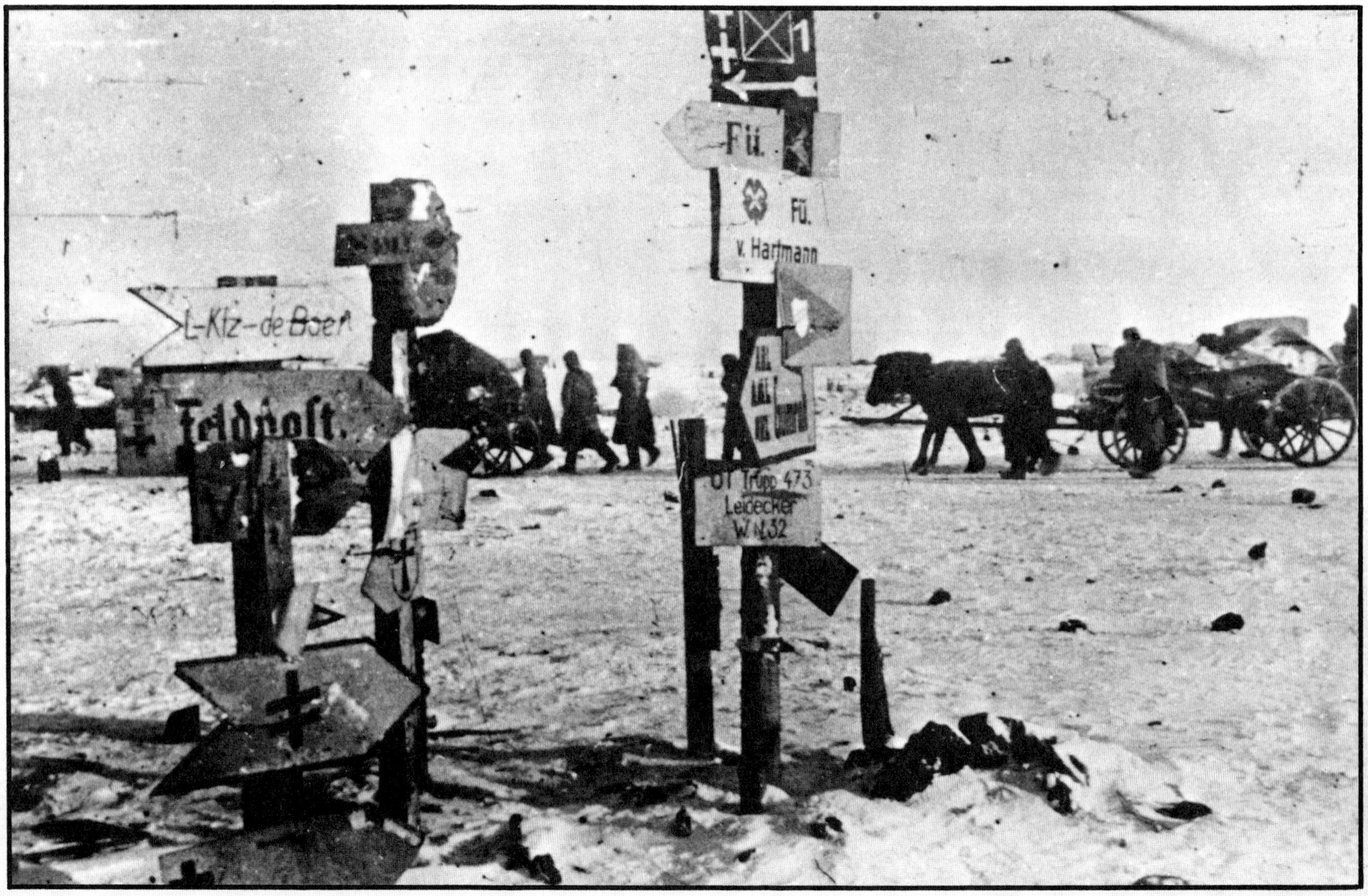
L-Kfz-de Boer
Feldpost.
Fü.
Fü.
v. Hartmann
OT Trupp 473
Leidecker
W.N.32

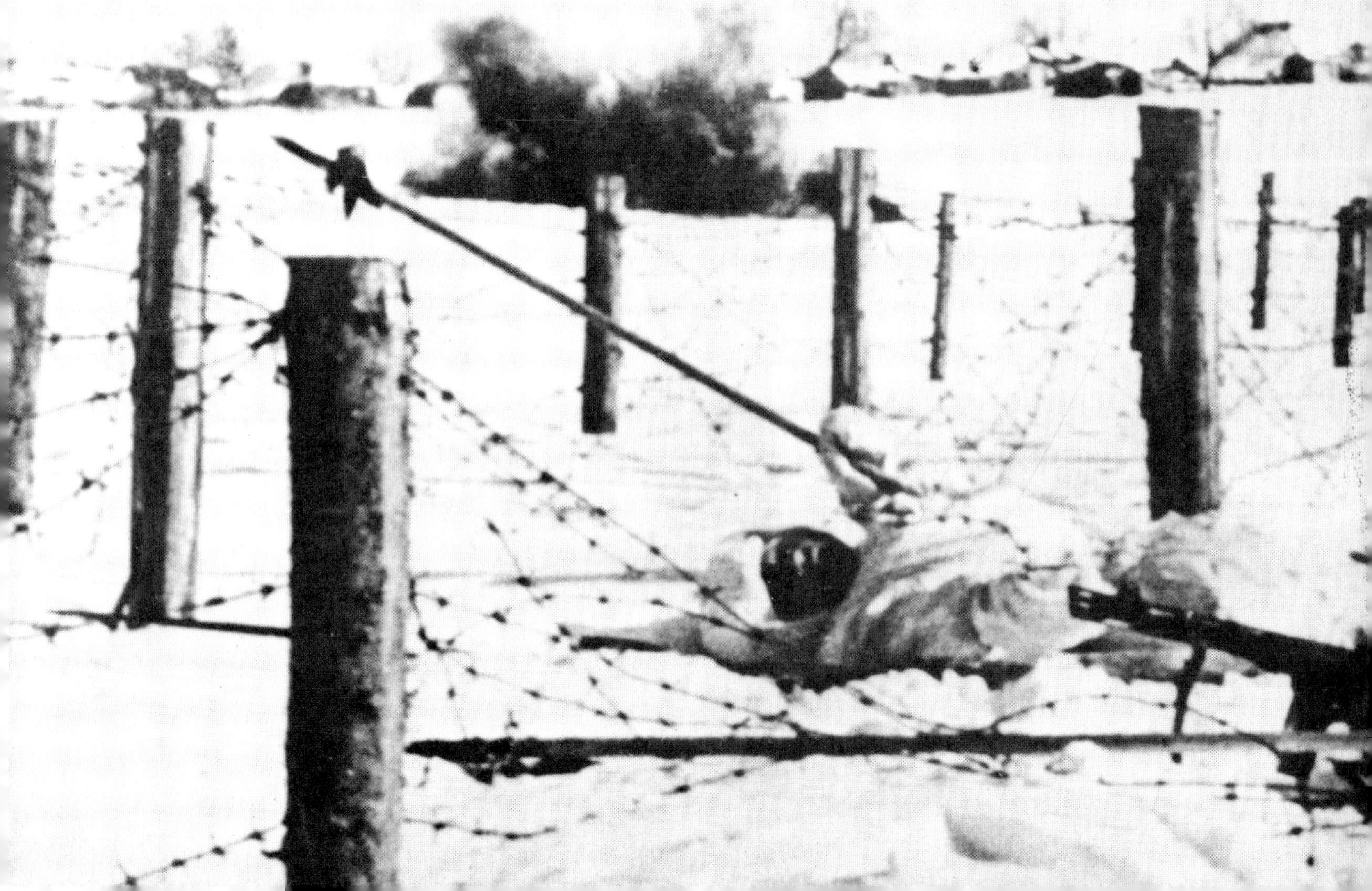

Left : **Russian forces pass abandoned German road signs during their counteroffensive in early 1943.**
Below : **German sappers cut Russian barbed wire in their attempt to re-establish a front west of Stalingrad in March 1943.**

At one stage some 300 men of the 295th Infantry Division raided the Russian rear on the Volga by crawling through a sewer pipe, but were wiped out. On 29 October Chuikov's headquarters was bombed and burning oil spilled over it; still all escaped from this blazing inferno alive. On 5 October Stalin ordered Yeremenko to keep Stalingrad at all costs, while Chuikov found a new headquarters, evacuated by the NKVD 10th Division which was withdrawn from the fighting after being decimated.

On 7 October Chuikov's planned counterattack never got off the ground, for two German divisions launched their own assault. In the heavy fighting which ensued the Germans lost some four battalions of dead and scores of tanks were wiped out. General Paulus ordered these suicidal attacks, as he was told by General Schmundt that a Field Marshal's baton was at the end of Stalingrad fighting. Paulus seemed quite ruthless about getting his baton – when fellow commanders objected to his way of handling the operations, they were dismissed: General von Wietersheim of the XV Panzer Corps and General von Schwendler of the IV Panzer Corps. Between 9 and 13 October a sort of lull settled over Stalingrad; fighting continued, but there were no large-scale attacks while the Wehrmacht regrouped and prepared for the final assault.

On Monday 14 October at 0800 hours three infantry divisions (94th, 389th and 100th) and two Panzer divisions (14th and 24th) hurled themselves onto the central sector of the town, surrounded the Tractor Factory and reached the Volga splitting Chuikov's army into two. Overnight Chuikov received reinforcements (138th Regiment), but even the fresh troops could not stop the German battering ram. On the following day the Germans overran the height, Mamaya Kurgan, and they penetrated the improvized Russian fortresses, the Krasny Oktyabr and Barrikady plants on the Volga itself. Only on 24 October could the Russians counterattack, skillfully using their artillery from the other side of the Volga, make any impact. The 45th Division was ferried over and it finally cleared the Germans from the Volga; by 29 October the Germans spent themselves and on the following day there were no attacks. All this time both in the south and north, Generals Shumilov's and Rokossovsky's relief attacks were beaten back and subdued.

Once again an uneasy lull settled over the city while street fighting continued

unabated. The Russians continued to ferry over fresh troops to replace casualties, while the Germans were running their men into the ground. On 11 November, after an artillery and Stuka bombardment, the Germans launched their last attack in the city. Casualties were high on both sides, but the Germans once again reached the Volga splitting Chuikov's forces for the third time. The city was in danger of falling into German hands, for by now Chuikov could not get any more reinforcements, as they were required elsewhere. In fact this German attack caused a crisis in Moscow at the Stavka (Supreme HQ), whose strategic offensive, planned and prepared throughout October, was now only a week from being launched. Chuikov had to survive a week without relief; by 20 November all offensive activity by the Wehrmacht in Stalingrad ceased. The Germans had to face the consequences of the Soviet strategic counteroffensive, Uranus.

As we have seen Hitler realized the dangers of a strategic offensive in the Don area in mid-August. Still by October he seemed to have forgotten these dangers and on 14 October issued his *Operationsbefehl No 1* in which he ordered all the offensive activity, except in Stalingrad and in the Caucasus, to cease, while the Wehrmacht prepared for winter defense; he promised to destroy the Red Army in 1943. The thinking behind this order is best exemplified in General Zeitzler's commentary in which it was claimed that no major Russian offensive was possible so late in 1942. In fact they were both wrong, for the Russians, ever since 12 September, when Generals Zhukov and Vasilievsky first spoke to Stalin about the "other solution," as distinct from the diversionary attacks north and south of Stalingrad, went ahead with their planning of a strategic offensive. Needless to say the operation was a top secret, which Stalin did not divulge even to Churchill, whom he entertained in Moscow late in August 1942. Even Russian commanders, among them General Yeremenko, were told nothing of the planning, so that Yeremenko later mistakenly claimed that he planned the counteroffensive, at least in his southern sector.

Zhukov and Vasilievsky worked out two plans of the strategic offensive: the one codenamed Saturn, which was the major breakthrough to Milerovo–Rostov feared so much by Hitler, and the other code-

Below: **A street in Kursk is cleared of rubble after the Russians retook the city and created a salient which the Germans attacked in June 1943.**

207

Left: **Russian paratroops provide the backdrop for a self-propelled gun west of Moscow during the 1943 Soviet offensive.** *Above:* **A Nazi soldier leaps from his burning tank as the Soviets close the trap.**

Above: **Germans had orders not to retreat and fear was used to insure that the German soldiers did not abandon their positions.**

named Uranus, which aimed at simultaneous breakthroughs in the north and south some 60 miles west of Stalingrad trapping the German armies on the Volga. It was the second variant which was adopted and planned to be launched on 9 November, possibly to coincide with Operation Torch, Allied landings in North Africa. Logistic problems delayed the offensive for a week but it was an extremely well planned and executed offensive. As early as September, when the fronts to carry out this offensive were formed, both Zhukov and Vasilievsky personally studied the terrain and the troops. On 22 October the newly established three fronts were finally told of Uranus. In the north the offensive would be carried out by the Southwestern Front under General Vatutin, who would have at his disposal the 1st Guards and 21st Armies, 5th Tank Army and would be covered by General Krasovsky's 17th Air Army. Vatutin would attack in conjunction with the newly formed Don Front under General Rokossovsky whose 24th, 65th and 66th Armies were to be covered by General Rudenko's 16th Air Army. In the south General Yeremenko's Stalingrad Front, also newly formed, would break through with 51st, 57th and 64th Armies spearheaded by General Volsky's IV Mechanized Corps. The two armies would close their pincers in the Kalach area. Zhukov and Vasilievsky went through the offensive tasks of all the fronts and armies in person with all the commanders, and still did not convince them that the offensive would be a success. On 17 November, rather late in the day, General Volsky felt it his duty as a party member to warn Stalin that his offensive in the south, in which he played a vital role, would fail. Stalin was most perturbed and asked his two commanders, Zhukov and Vasilievsky, to explain Volsky's complaint: when they could not, Stalin telephoned Volsky to go into the offensive despite his lack of conviction, for it could not be called off or postponed. For Operation Uranus the Russians amassed some 1,000,500 men, 13,541 guns, 894 tanks and 1115 aircraft, in order to break the two flanks held by badly equipped Rumanians, 3rd Army and VI Corps respectively. Given the wrong intelligence evaluation and bad meteorological conditions which prevented the Luftwaffe from reconnoitering, Uranus was the greatest surprise attack ever to hit the Wehrmacht.

On 19 November at midnight snow clouds arrived over the northern sector and freezing fog enveloped all. Still the artillery barrage started as planned at 0730 hours. At 0850 hours the infantry and tanks went into action and soon began to overwhelm the Rumanians who were fighting most valiantly. Hitler in his HQ at Vinnitsa, which was in even greater darkness than the battlefield, ordered General Heim's XLVIII Panzer Corps to counterattack

Left: **Soviet planes and tanks press forward repelling an attack of the Waffen-SS during the Battle of Kursk.**

Above: **Peasant girl gives Soviet soldiers some liquid encouragement during their drive westwards.**
Left: **Soviet T-34s roll off the assembly line as Russian tank production outstripped German armored production by the end of 1943.**
Below left: **Soviet infantry drive forward during the long German retreat.**

towards Kletskaya, but the Russian tanks were not there. Heim had to turn to face General Romanenko's 5th Tank Army which emerged from the snowy darkness pulverizing all in its path. General Radu's 1st Rumanian Armored Division, without communication with HQ, was lost in the snow and drove to its doom without realizing it. After this catastrophe Romanenko's tanks caused panic among the Rumanian infantry. The breakthrough was achieved and the tanks began to pour south leaving the infantry to do the mopping up and secure the flanks. Late that day Hitler ordered Paulus to break off attacks in Stalingrad and plug the hole in his northern flank. He had no idea that another hole would be punched in the German southern flank.

On 20 November fog delayed Yeremenko's offensive only slightly: the barrage started at 1000 hours and forty minutes later the tanks and infantry went into action. When the tanks caught up with them the VI Rumanian Corps surrendered and the Fourth Panzers had to withdraw in a hurry to avoid encirclement. Two days later Volsky's advance reached Sovetsky and forced the German headquarters to disperse: Hitler ordered Paulus to fly back to his headquarters at Gumrak-Stalingrad thus sealing the fate of the General and his armies. On 23 November at 1400 hours the two Russian pincers linked and Hitler proclaimed the encircled Sixth Army and Fourth Panzer Army as *Festung* Stalingrad, a fortress, rather than permit the armies to break out of the encirclement, which at this stage would have been possible. However when Reichsmarschall Goering assured Hitler that the Luftwaffe could supply the encircled armies, he decided that Paulus should hold out until relief operations could be organized. Some 270,000 men were in the trap and the Russians almost immediately launched their "chop up operation" against them.

Hitler also initiated the relief action almost immediately, but there would be another surprise in store for him, when the Russians launched Operation (Little) Saturn. Field Marshal von Manstein was called from Vitebsk to the Don and given the task of organizing a new relief army. On 24 November, when he arrived at Starobelsk he found the railway system disorganized and often unusable due to partisan activity, with no forces to form the new army and counsels divided: both Paulus and the Army Group B wanted to break out from the encirclement. However Hitler overruled them and Manstein decided to relieve Stalingrad from the southwest with the invigorated Fourth Panzer Army. However General Balck's 11th Panzers who were coming up from Rostov to the Chir, where the breakthrough was to start, ran into Russian tanks and had to fight in order to advance to the starting line. Blizzards raged over the Don area, men and vehicles were lost; snow delayed the 57th Panzers, too. On 12 December Manstein launched his relief operation with insufficient forces and badly prepared. Russian diversionary attacks soon slowed down his progress and he sent Major Eismann to Paulus to ask him to break through in order to help the relieving force. However both Paulus and Hitler refused to break out and Manstein inevitably ran out of steam. He lost most of his armor and in the subsequent retreat most of his infantry. All this time Hitler had at his disposal large forces in the Crimea and even in the Caucasus where the offensive was also stuck and could not be resumed. Then on 16 December General Golikov's Voronezh Front smashed the Eighth Italian Army thus setting into motion Operation Saturn. If Milerovo and Rostov were reached as a result of this breakthrough, the disaster on the Eastern front in 1942 would be complete.

Nothing could save Paulus at Stalingrad. On 8 January 1943 General Rokossovsky demanded Paulus's surrender, but it was refused because the men were convinced that the Russians would not stick to the honorable treatment they promised. Four days later Rokossovsky launched a concentric assault on the city, gained some five miles of the perimeter and more significantly took the airfield at Pitomnik through which most German supplies trickled in. Paulus, who was made Field Marshal in his defeat, contained the attack, but the Russians renewed it and on 23 January the last airstrip at Gumrak was under Russian control. The Germans were driven into the ruins of the town, where they surrendered after another week of desperate fighting; with Paulus, 24 generals and some 92,000 men went into captivity. Ironically hardly any of them survived, not because the Russians practiced on them the *Einsatzgruppen* techniques, but because of their generally weak condition which coupled with the inhospitable climate and disease wiped out most of the men, though not their officers.

While Manstein failed to save Paulus and Stalingrad, he did save the Caucasian Front armies. In January 1943 when Hitler finally gave orders to withdraw from the Caucasus, it was rather late and the Russians began to converge on Rostov from two directions. If they could reach Rostov, General von Kleist, who succeeded Field Marshal List, would have been cut off and his First Panzer Army and the Seventeenth Armies lost. It was a race against time as Kleist extricated his troops harrassed by partisans and Soviet aircraft, and nevertheless managed to slip through the Rostov gap, which Manstein kept open for him. On 6 February 1943 Hitler invited Manstein to a conference, at which Hitler not only accepted all the blame and responsibility for Stalingrad, but also gave him permission to withdraw to the Mius river line. Two years previously the mere suggestion of such a solution had cost Rundstedt his command. Moreover Kleist, after the completion of his successful retreat, received from Hitler the Field Marshal's baton.

Far left : **Another German submarine is launched to continue the Battle of the Atlantic.**
Left : **Grand Admiral Raeder was the head of the Kriegsmarine until his replacement by Karl Doenitz as the Battle of the Atlantic heightened.**
Right : **The petty officers' quarters on the** *U-995*, **a late model built in 1943.**
Below right : **The depth regulator area on an early model U-Boat.**
Below : **The** *U-203* **as it left Brest for mid-Atlantic waters in 1943, when the Germans almost cut supply lines between Britain and America.**

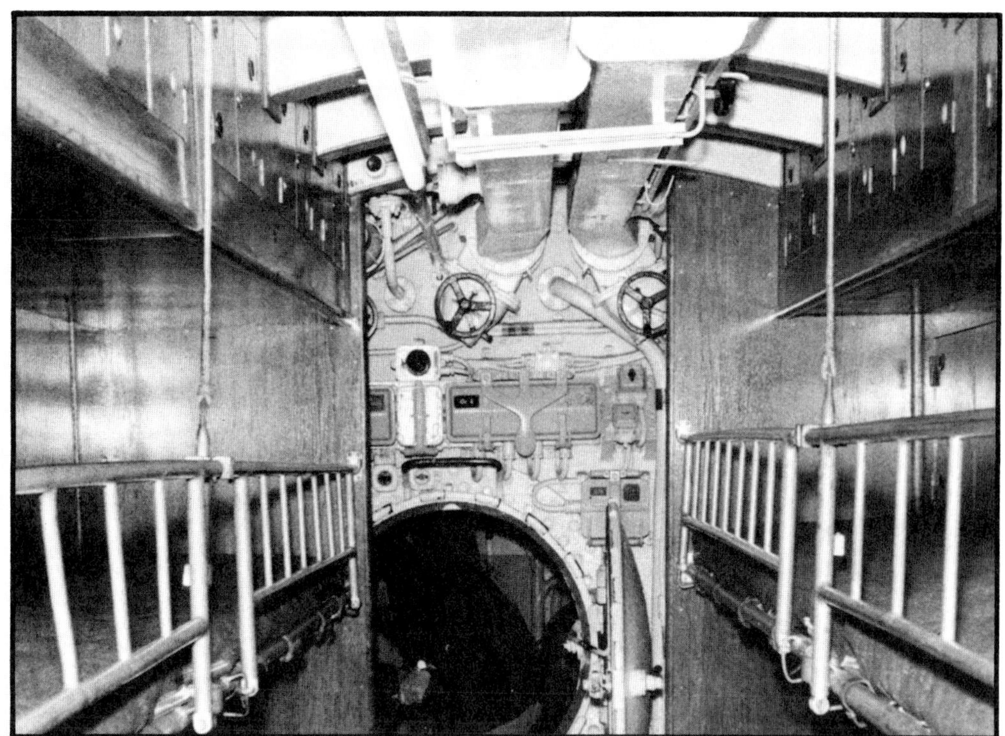

Far left: **Men of *U-86* on the lookout for Allied shipping.**
Center left: **Wolf packs on the prowl.**
Left: **The Naval Hitler Youth attends a rally at Berlin's Sportspalast in 1943.**
Below: **American naval personnel capture *U-505*, which is now on display at Chicago's Museum of Science and Industry.**
Bottom: **Grand Admiral Karl Doenitz reviews U-Boat crews before they prowled the Atlantic waters.**

Apart from throwing away some 250,000 men Hitler lost initiative on the Eastern Front and never really regained it. By the end of February 1943 German front lines had moved some 200 miles west and Hitler could not even make his armies fight the same successful defense battles as in the previous winter. The Wehrmacht lacked men and armor for such a defense, while the Russians seem to have learned all the lessons of tank warfare: the fronts were very fluid and Hitler seemed lost, but all the same he allowed Guderian to control the armor in the south and fight defensive battles, to save Kharkov. On 21 February Hoth's armor attacked Popov and the 3rd SS Panzer Division equipped with new

Below: *U-826*, **flying the British white ensign, and** *U-236* **after they gave themselves up to the Royal Navy.**
Above right: **US aircraft drop bombs over Kassel as the air offensive over Germany heightened.**

Tiger tanks broke through the Russian line of advance. When their pincers closed, they captured some 9000 Russians, but still most of them escaped across the frozen Donets. But even this flexible defense failed to save Kharkov, which was evacuated without a fight, and the German front line came to rest almost exactly in the same place as it had been in 1942, when the Germans launched their summer offensive.

While the fronts stabilized until July 1943 the Germans could not relax. Large partisan armies increased their activity and the Wehrmacht instead of resting had to hunt for these enemies in its rear. In January and February 1943 Operations *Eisbär* I, II and III were launched against partisans in the areas of Bryansk, Dmitriyev and Mikhailovka. In these operations the Wehrmacht was aided by a Russian militia force commanded by a tough collaborator, Kaminsky. In Operations *Erntefest* I and II, police and SS formations had to help out in Belorussia. But in the area Kletnya and Mamyevka (Operations *Klette* I and II) the Wehrmacht had to do all the dirty work entailed by anti-partisan operations on its own. By March and May 1943 these large-scale operations were given more and more lyrical names [*Ursula* I, II; *Winterzauber* (Wintermagic), *Zauberflöte* (Magic Flute), *Zigeunerbaron* (Gypsy Baron), *Freischütz* (Magic Marksmanship)], but were the same depressing

Left: **The ball-bearing plant at Schweinfurt, which was a principal target for Allied aircraft in 1943. Some 400 Luftwaffe planes were shot down during the ten air raids over Schweinfurt.** *Right:* **Bombs drop over Schweinfurt during the October 1943 raids.**

reality: massacres of civilian population and the burning of villages. However the Wehrmacht's behavior on retreat did not much differ from these punitive expeditions – the Germans left behind utter and complete devastation.

In the meantime the Western Allies also prepared for a blow to the German military power. Though Stalin goaded them throughout the year 1942 to start a second front in France, they did not feel sufficiently strong to carry it out, especially after the British had been repulsed at Dieppe. Following Field Marshal Rommel's victories in Libya and Egypt Premier Churchill persuaded President Roosevelt to launch Operation Torch, which meant that British and American troops would land in Northwestern Africa: Casablanca, Oran and Algiers. The Free French were not told much and therefore there was initial resistance; in retaliation Hitler ordered German troops to occupy the rest of France and also seize airfields and sea ports in Tunisia. This act of German "perfidy" convinced the French, especially Admiral Darlan who was in Algiers by chance, that they must co-operate with the Allies. However before co-operation could proceed further Darlan was assassinated and General de Gaulle was able to take over: General Juin was to lead French armies into Tunisia with the Americans and British. Hitler also tried to seize the French fleet at Toulon but Admiral Laborde preferred to scuttle it. Although needing German troops in the USSR Hitler poured men into Northern Africa only to suffer another disastrous defeat.

Rommel launched his final offensive against Egypt on 1 July 1942, three days after Hitler's offensive on the Eastern Front. But there were no spectacular breakthroughs for Rommel at El Alamein: British defenses and then armor withstood the first assault and inflicted irreplaceable losses on him. For the rest of July fierce fighting continued while both sides were rushing reinforcements to El Alamein. General Auchinleck, who had numerical superiority over the Germans and Italians throughout, especially in tanks, only managed to halt Rommel's advance, but failed to defeat him. Premier Churchill then flew to Cairo and replaced Auchinleck with General Montgomery; however at the battle of Alam Halfa Montgomery delivered the same indecisive results as Auchinleck. Still the Royal Air Force began to blast Rommel's tanks which were handicapped by inadequate oil supplies, out of the desert; early in September 1942 Rommel started his tactical retreat. The British were in turn preparing their final offensive.

For this offensive the 8th Army mustered some 230,000 men, 1440 tanks and 1200 aircraft. By then Rommel only had some 80,000 men and 260 German and 280 Italian tanks with some 350 serviceable aircraft. However the Germans lacked oil, because their supply ships were being sunk and troops suffered from dysentery and jaundice – even Rommel was sick and returned to Germany for treatment. His replacement, General Stumme, died of a heart attack two days after the British offensive started. On 25 October 1942, the very day of the offensive, Rommel flew back from Austria to take charge of operations and soon had the British in trouble. But he had insufficient forces to resist the British assault, though even there Hitler ordered him not to withdraw. Only on 3 November did Montgomery's forces break through and they could have trapped the whole of Rommel's *Afrika Korps* had they exploited the advantage properly. Rommel was allowed to retreat successfully losing Benghazi on 20 November and Tripoli on 23 January 1943. By then he had reached General Jürgen von Arnim's Fifth Army which Hitler transferred to Tunisia to defend it against the Allies from Algeria.

After the successful Torch landings in November 1942 Allied armies intended to invade Tunisia: the British 1st Army along the coast to Tunis; while the American II Corps and French XIX Corps would move further south. The 1st Army was easily checked by the Germans who had only recently landed and enjoyed air superiority. In the south the French were heavily mauled while the inexperienced Americans were cut to pieces on 14 February 1943. However by now Rommel was at loggerheads with von Arnim and they failed to exploit this victory. Later in February and early in March 1943 Rommel unleashed his Fifth Army on the British 1st and 8th Armies, blooding their noses though suffering unacceptable losses in turn. Three days after his attack on the British at Medenine Rommel had to retire to Germany because of sickness, leaving Air Field Marshal Kesselring in command.

However both the British and Americans recovered from their surprise and launched attacks against the Mareth line, an improvized defense which protected the Germans and Italians in Tunisia. General Patton, who took command of the II Corps, attacked in the direction of Gafsa, while Montgomery's 8th Army tried to break the Mareth Line frontally. In the end New Zealanders outflanked the Germans who were forced to retire by the end of March. Next the Italian First Army was put under combined Anglo-American pressure and by 6 April 1943 it also withdrew towards Tunis. Throughout April 1943 the British 1st Army and the American II Corps pushed on towards Tunis which finally fell on 7 May. The Germans and Italians continued their resistance for another week, "until the last shot," when they surrendered: Hitler had thrown away another 275,000 men for no advantage at all.

Before the Western Allies could chastise Germany in the Mediterranean by landing in Sicily, Hitler was humbled by the Soviet armies on the Eastern Front. He now concentrated his attention entirely on the east, but this time without grandiose strategic plans. He thought most feverishly of new weapons and charged Guderian with revitalizing the Panzer forces. He no longer planned strategic offensives but did sanction the only large offensive in the summer of 1943, *Fall Zitadelle*. Paradoxically Hitler's very abstention from interfering in the planning condemned the offensive to failure, for in 1943 he was the only man who knew the complete strategic situation on the Eastern Front. *Zitadelle* or Citadel was a two-pronged attack on the Kursk salient and became the greatest tank battle of World War II. General Zeitzler planned the attack with two Army Groups under Field Marshals von Kluge and von Manstein, but General Jodl was against the offensive, for he wanted to preserve reserves in case they were needed in the Mediterranean area. General Guderian also wanted to wait until 1944 as he would have only some 324 Panther tanks for the offensive. Thus throughout the planning stage there was no unity of views, plenty of differences, hopeless hesitations and a complete lack of reliable intelligence on Soviet intentions.

Above: **Marienburg, Germany under air attack.**

The Russians could also see that the Germans would counterattack in the Kursk area and in contrast to the Germans they prepared well for the attack. Above all they were bringing in armor and guns at a greater speed than the Germans who were to attack. On the Central front under Rokossovsky's command there were five armies in the front line and the 2nd Tank Army behind them. Vatutin's Voronezh front also had five armies deployed and the 1st Tank Army to back them in the flank of the salient. Moreover the Stavka built

Left: **Armament Minister Albert Speer talks with a French colleague. Speer's organization of war production prolonged the war for at least a year.**

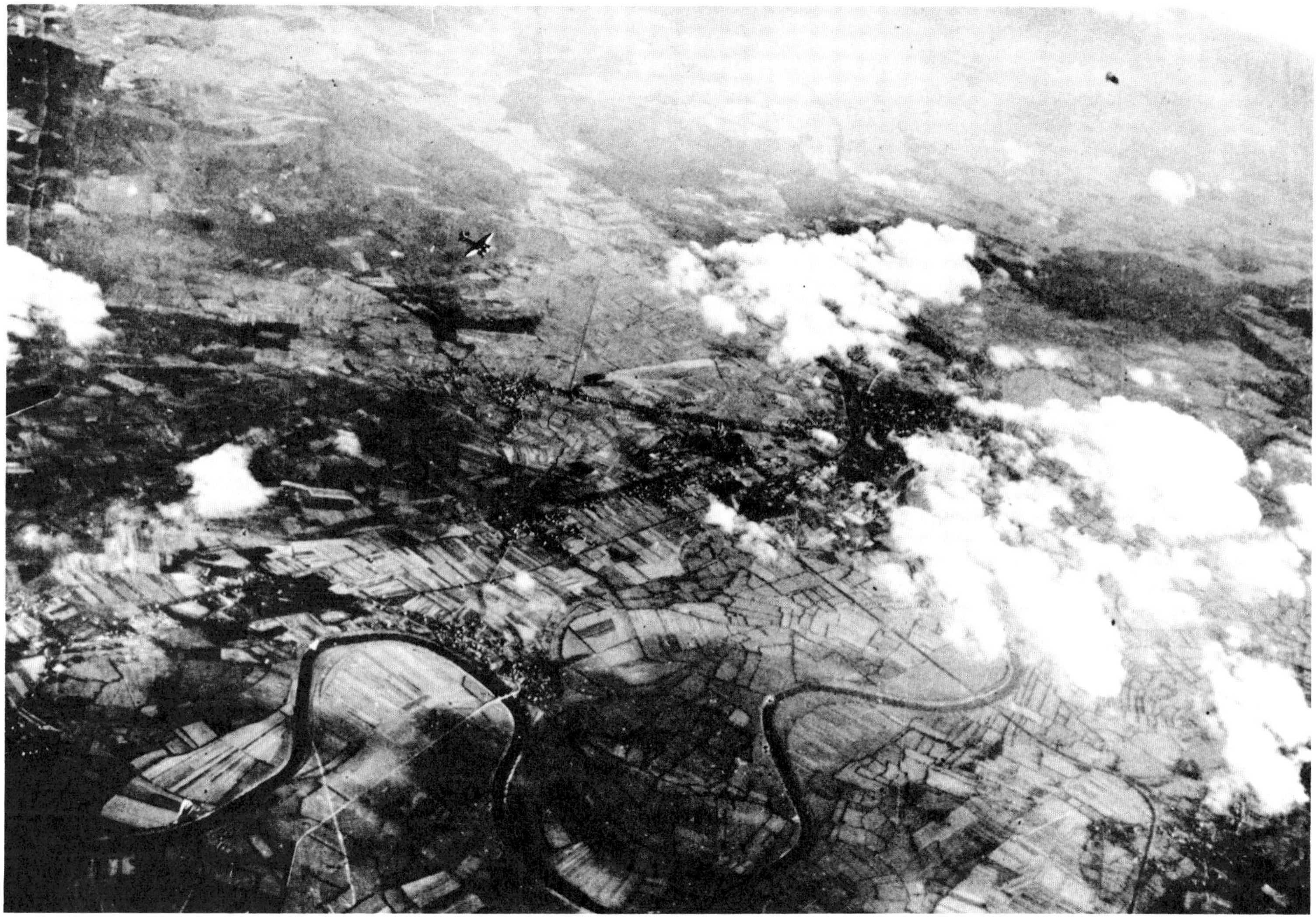

Above : **B-17s in the air battle over Bremen.**

up its strategic reserve there in the form of the Steppe front under the command of General Ivan Konev, who commanded three armies and the 5th Guards Tank Army. The salient was also well fortified with trenches in three zones and had extensive minefields. Thus the German Fourth Panzer Army, which was to attack in the south and the Ninth Army which was attacking in the north, were heading for the most terrifying rebuff ever administered to German armies. They would fall into a well-prepared trap.

On 4 July 1943 the Wehrmacht went on the offensive once again. Immediately many German tanks were immobilized by mines, but their wedge-like advance proved successful and the first line of Russian defenses was taken. However the Germans suffered heavy losses and Guderian's fears were proved right: the new Panther tanks were insufficiently protected and were easily set ablaze, because their crews were not properly trained. The Ninth Army used the Ferdinand self-propelled tanks which again the infantry could not protect and Soviet infantrymen managed to climb up on them and use their flamethrowers against engine ventilation slots. In any case Russian armor was moving up during the night and the Germans had to face the same odds as when they started. Still in the next five days they fought hard, especially the élite SS formations, *Grossdeutschland, Das Reich, Leibstandarte* and *Totenkopf,* which were best equipped, and succeeded in denting the Russian defenses both in the north and the south. However General Sokolovsky's Western Front then counterattacked on the extended left flank of the Ninth Army and forced it to withdraw. On 12 July the Stavka committed its 5th Guards Tank Army equipped with the latest SU85 guns, which collided with General Hoth's Fourth Panzers and swept them back. The following day Hitler can-

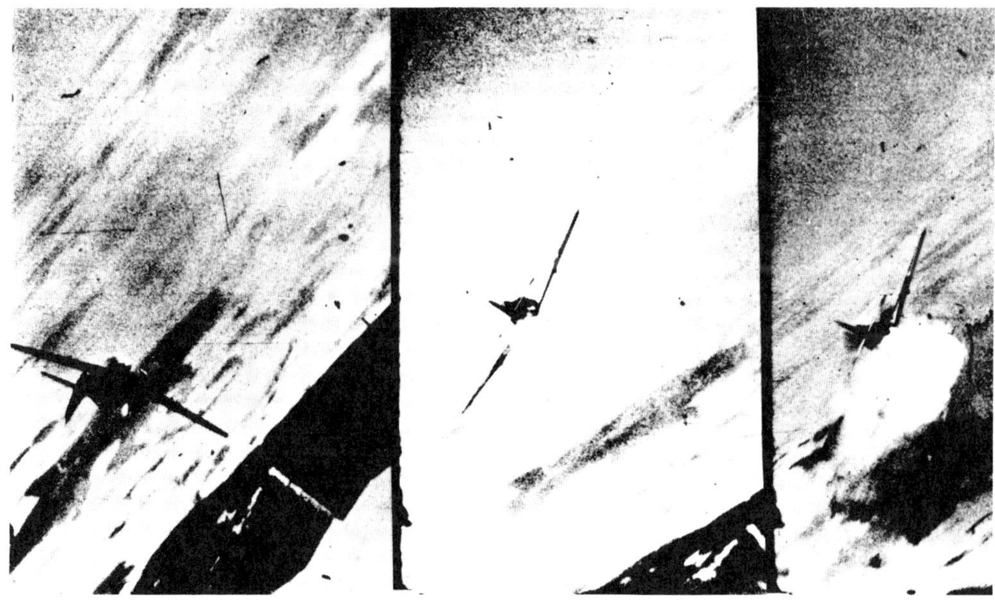

Right : **Three views of a Focke-Wulf 190 during an air battle with a North American P-51 Mustang in which the German aircraft was shot down.**

as a result the Germans lost some 20 divisions – 100,000 Germans went into captivity.

Russian penetrations into Poland during the month of July 1944 excited the Poles so much that they rose against the German garrison in Warsaw and by 6 August controlled most of the city. It seems that the Red Army genuinely ran out of steam in front of Warsaw, but Stalin also had ideological reasons for not making one more desperate effort to relieve the city: the uprising was organized from London and he had different political plans for Poland which obviously did not coincide with those of the London Poles. Hitler ordered the merciless suppression of the uprising and the destruction of the city; he transferred SS formations under SS Obergruppenführer Erich von dem Bach-Zelewski to the city and they hammered the city to smithereens. Former Soviet prisoners of war and German criminals on probation proved particularly ruthless and the uprising was quashed with terror. Still fighting continued for almost three months while the Russians seemingly did nothing. On 16 September 1944 the Polish division under General Zymierski was sent to relieve the city and though it reached the suburb Praga it could not move farther. As a result the Polish insurgents under General Bór surrendered to the Germans, who after their victory at Arnhem felt the surrender of Warsaw was another tremendous morale booster.

Despite these German victories the next collapse followed in the Balkans. By October 1944 the Russians aided by the Rumanian Army, cleared Transylvania of the Germans and prepared for the occupation of the Balkans by Malinovsky's and Tolbukhin's armies, some 38 divisions. While the 4th Ukrainian Front descended into Ruthenia and General Petrov's forces invaded Slovakia, Tolbukhin's armor crossed the Bulgarian border and on 11 September the new "patriotic front" government signed an armistice. At the same time the German front suddenly collapsed in Hungary and Malinovsky's 64 divisions drove fast to Budapest which they reached on 4 November 1944. Previously Belgrade was liberated and the Russian armies stood firm on the Danube.

It seemed clear that the German armies which were still in Greece and Yugoslavia would be cut off from Germany and destroyed. To extricate these precious troops from the Balkan trap Hitler sent Field Marshal von Weichs there, who only ordered the long retreat from Greece in November 1944. Throughout the winter months German armies defended themselves successfully against the various partisans and succeeded in breaking out from the Balkans. Another field marshal, Schörner, however, proved much less successful in the Baltic provinces and by the end of 1944 some 200,000 excellent German troops were isolated there. However the fronts again stabilized and Hitler quickly decided to

strike a deadly blow against the Allies in the West. Against the advice of his generals he concentrated some 20 divisions with 1000 tanks in the Ardennes area and decided to risk the outcome of the war on this desperate operation. In December 1944, when Hitler launched his offensive, the Russians were also ready to start their "usual" winter push forward, that front needed attention and required reserves which were being "wasted" in the West.

On 16 December the well-prepared Germans hurled themselves on the surprised 1st American Army. The Allies ignored intelligence reports of German concentrations in the area, for no one thought that the Germans were capable of an offensive on such a scale. Though Rundstedt was appointed Commander-in-Chief in the West, Hitler conducted this operation in person. He wanted to overwhelm the inexperienced Americans, separate them from the British in the north and then strike at their supply bases, even reach Antwerp. The Sixth SS Panzer Army was to play the vital role in this offensive although gasoline supplies were far from secure; after a while General Hasso von Manteuffel's Fifth Panzer Army inherited this rôle, when it had successfully broken the front. On 17 December Manteuffel's forces broke through in the Schnee Eifel area and captured some 8000 Americans. However, in the southern sector the Germans were checked and General Patton strengthened his front. In the north the advance was also checked after initial successes. Battle Group Peiper moved forward almost to the Meuse massacring American prisoners of war and Belgian civilians as it went. The deepest penetration was achieved in the central sector where Manteuffel's tanks cut off Bastogne on 10 December.

However 20 December seemed to have been the turning point of the offensive, albeit German armored advance still continued. It was on that day that General Collins's Americans turned south and checked the advance of the 15th German Panzer Grenadiers. Four days later, after the SS Panzers failed to reach the Peiper force, it had to abandon its tanks which ran out of fuel and retreat on foot back to the German line. On 26 December the Americans managed to relieve Bastogne and the Germans began to fall back all along the breakthrough. Dietrich's SS Panzers failed to help Manteuffel's Panzers as they both ran out of fuel, and since Hitler refused to give orders to retreat, he made quite sure that the offensive completely miscarried and needless heavy losses were incurred. Although the Allied advance was checked for months the Ardennes offensive insured the success of the Russian offensive, since by January 1945 Hitler had no reserves left with which to plug the holes which the Russians were going to punch in his eastern front.

Hitler's new Chief of Staff, General Guderian, anticipated the Russian offensive immediately after the Ardennes offensive and concentrated some twelve Panzer divisions to meet it. As early as 23 December Guderian requested that the Ardennes offensive be stopped and asked for the forces to be transferred to the East. Hitler refused all his requests, including tactical withdrawals in Poland and East Prussia so that a flexible defense could be put into

Left: **Soviet troops dance in the streets after the liberation of Lvov. After the Liberation Polish Communists tried to dominate the country and the Polish underground was involved in fighting until the Red Army suppressed them.**

Above: **US troops enter a Nazi stronghold in Germany in 1945.**

Below: **SS General von dem Bach-Zelewski greets his opponent in the Warsaw Uprising, General Bor-Komorowski, after resistance ended and the city was leveled in November 1944.**

operation. Guderian who toured the front in the first week of January 1945 was most impressed by the numerical increases of Russian forces all along this front: on the five fronts led by the best Russian generals, Chernyakhovsky, Rokossovsky, Zhukov, Konev and Petrov, Stalin had amassed some 225 infantry divisions and 22 armored corps and hoped to capture Upper Silesia and get to the river Oder. To face this mighty power Guderian had only twelve mechanized and some 50 infantry divisions.

On 12 January 1945 the Russians let loose their armies on Guderian's. Five days later Warsaw was finally taken, by

Left: **A German tank trap outside Berlin which was by-passed by the Soviets in the spring of 1945.**
Below: **A German woman looks at the ruins of her home as US troops pass through Bönnigheim in March 1945.**

which time Zhukov's armored spearhead reached Lódź and Krakow. By 19 January both cities were taken, the Red Army was on the threshold of Silesia and East Prussia: the Russian advance was 100 miles deep over some 400 miles. Within two weeks of fighting the Russians took 113,000 prisoners, invested Königsberg and finally fought on German soil. The long awaited Russian revenge was at hand, but Hitler still did everything his own way. He refused Guderian's request for the evacuation of 26 divisions in the Baltic states and diverted Dietrich's SS Sixth Panzer Army to Hungary instead of the Polish front. By now Zhukov had reached Pomerania and Brandenburg, Konev isolated Upper Silesia and the Red Army devastated the occupied East Prussia which was not properly evacuated.

By the end of February 1945 when the Russians again outran their supplies, Konev took Katovice, crossed the upper Oder, invested Breslau, reached Sommerfeld on his oblique way to Berlin and came to a halt on the Neisse river. Zhukov, who had as his objective the German capital, by-passed Poznań, took Landsberg, invested Küstrin and was checked on the Oder. On 23 February the Russians finally took Poznań, while ten days earlier they had taken Budapest with 110,000 German prisoners. The scale of Russian victories completely unhinged Guderian, who began to quarrel with Hitler. On 8 February Hitler almost hit his Chief of Staff, while five days later Guderian had to listen to Hitler's raging and ranting for two hours. Still he forced the Führer to allow General Wenck to assist Reichsführer Himmler in the preparation of a counterattack at Amswalde. Himmler without military experience was bound to bungle the job, but Hitler seemed to have boundless confidence in him. The six Panzer divisions which Guderian had ready for the offensive were too weak, especially since the tank crews were either exhausted or inexperienced. They also lacked air support and were counterattacking in the wrong place: the mass of the 47th Russian Army was farther back. Moreover Wenck, who had to attend Hitler's briefings, crashed on his way back to the front and being seriously wounded could not lead the

Below: **German women and children flee the blazing ruins of their homes in Kronach.**
Bottom: **German refugees flee westward to be liberated by the Western Allies.**

counterattack. After four days the Germans had to give up. Hitler subsequently sacked Guderian and replaced him with General Krebs, the erstwhile military attaché in Moscow.

By the end of February, after the Russians had ceased to hammer Germany, the Allies dropped their political superbomb on Germany from Yalta, where they were meeting to divide the world among themselves after the defeat of Germany, which now seemed a foregone conclusion. The principle of unconditional surrender was upheld, and the Russians were allowed a zone of influence in Eastern Europe as well as in Germany. The Germans, how-

Left: **German Prisoners of War are used to clear and reconstruct damaged airfields.**
Below: **British forces liberate a Dutch town prior to the Allied crossing of the Rhine.**

ever, only heard rumors of these proceedings which confirmed Hitler in his determination to fight to the last. Goebbels made a great propaganda coup with the leaked Morgenthau Plan which envisaged the dismantling of German industry after the war, but really needed no more to add to the horrors of Bolshevism, the specter which now haunted Germany itself. In this final phase Hitler turned to Goebbels, who, after General Guderian and Minister Speer had disappointed him, was practically the only Nazi leader sharing his Führer's belief in the hopeless alternative: victory or *Götterdämmerung*.

It was the turn of the Western Allies to

Right: **US "dogface" inspects a vehicle during the advance through Germany.**
Below: **The "dragons' teeth" of a tank trap is by-passed by US troops near Roetgen as the "impregnable" Siegfried Line in penetrated.**

bring forward Hitler's death wish. The Russian winter offensive denuded the Western Front and the Allies prepared a veritable battering ram to get across the Rhine and invade Germany proper. The main rôle this time went to General Montgomery's group of armies, the 1st Canadian Army, the 2nd British Army and the 9th American Army. Still it was the Americans who had started the movements on the fronts. On 7 March General Patton's tanks broke through the German line in the Eifel hills and three days later reached the Rhine near Koblenz. Farther north at Remagen elements of General Bradley's armies captured a bridge across the Rhine intact, but failed to exploit it on the direct orders of Generalissimo Eisenhower. By 21 March a stretch of 70 miles on the western bank of the Rhine was clear of German forces, but the Americans waited for Montgomery's attack before plunging into Germany. On 23 March Montgomery launched his attack with 25 divisions against five dispirited German divisions and soon had bridgeheads on the other side of the Rhine; Germany's Western Front was ready to collapse.

In Italy German collapse was also imminent. In April 1945 when the 8th Army

Below: **US troops cross the Rhine in a "duck" barge specially constructed for the purpose.**

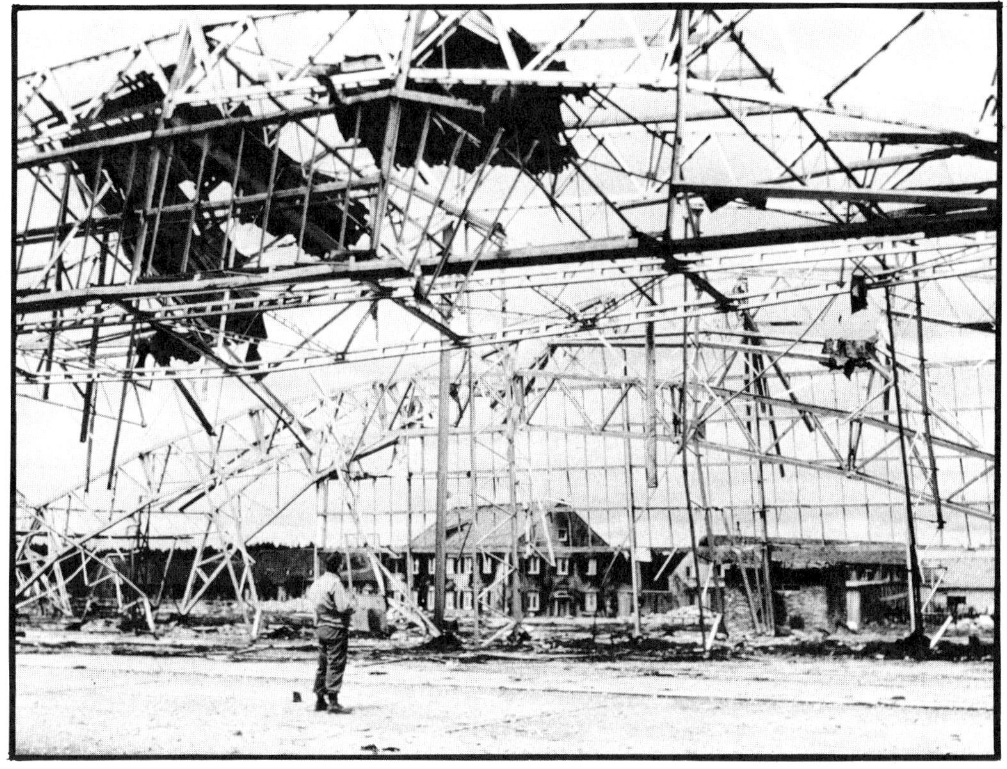

Above: **A bombed-out repair shop and hangar of the Dornier aircraft factory at Oberpfaffenhofen near Munich.**

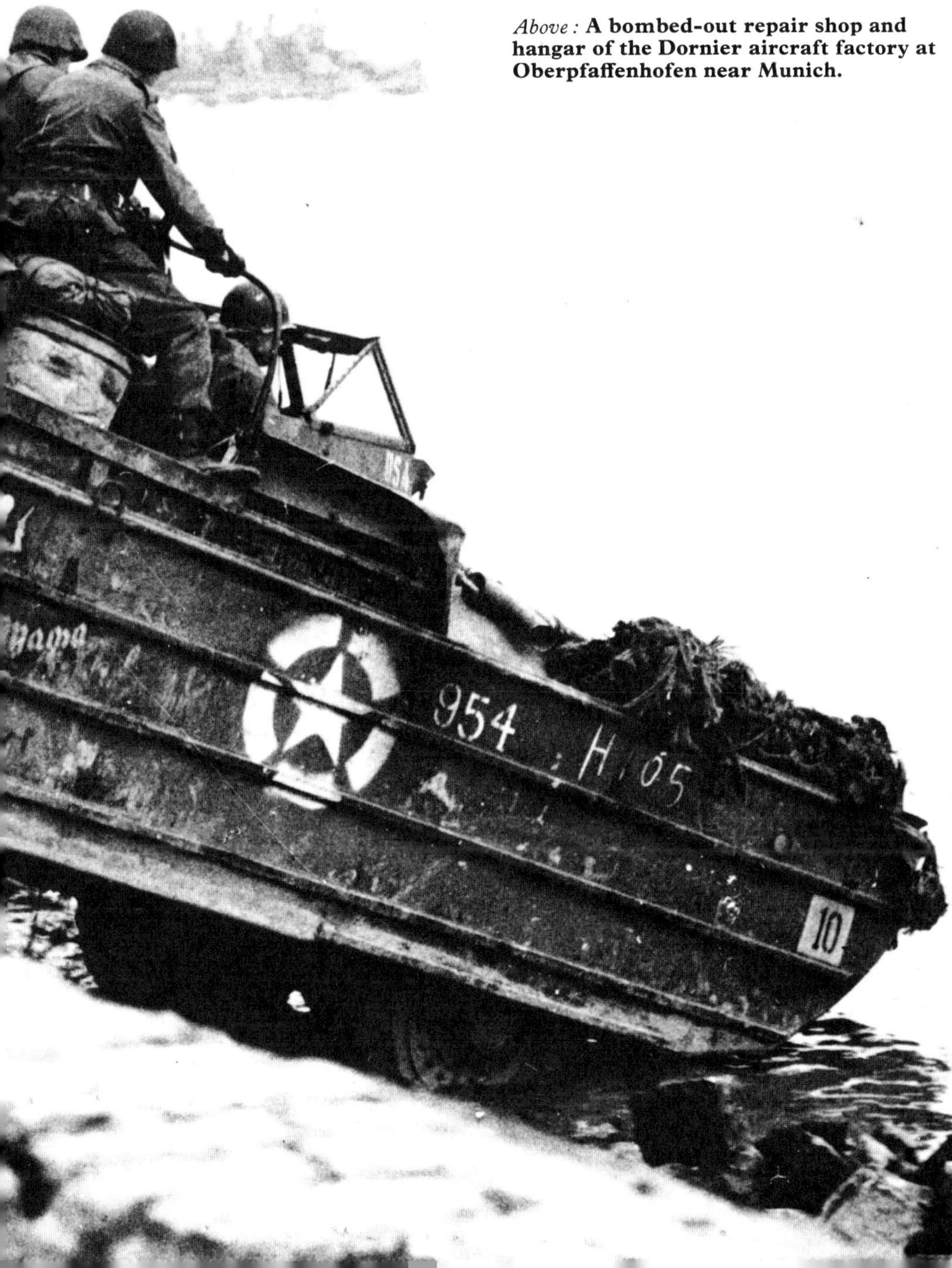

Führer Order

Order of the Day 15 April 1945.

Soldiers of the German Eastern front!
For the last time our deadly enemies the Jewish Bolsheviks have launched their massive forces to the attack. Their aim is to reduce Germany to ruins and to exterminate our people. Many of you soldiers in the East already know the fate which threatens, above all, German women, girls, and children. While the old men and children will be murdered, the women and girls will be reduced to barrack-room whores. The remainder will be marched off to Siberia.

We have foreseen this thrust, and since last January have done everything possible to construct a strong front. The enemy will be greeted by massive artillery fire. Gaps in our infantry have been made good by countless new units. Our front is being strengthened by emergency units, newly raised units, and by the Volkssturm. This time the Bolshevik will meet the ancient fate of Asia – he must and shall bleed to death before the capital of the German Reich. Whoever fails in his duty at this moment behaves as a traitor to our people. The regiment or division which abandons its position acts so disgracefully that it must be ashamed before the women and children who are withstanding the terror of bombing in our cities. Above all, be on your guard against the few treacherous officers and soldiers who, in order to preserve their pitiful lives, fight against us in Russian pay, perhaps even wearing German uniform. Anyone ordering you to retreat will, unless you know him well personally, be immediately arrested and, if necessary, killed on the spot, no matter what rank he may hold. If every soldier on the Eastern Front does his duty in the days and weeks which lie ahead, the last assault of Asia will crumple, just as the invasion by our enemies in the West will finally fail, in spite of everything.

Berlin remains German, Vienna will be German again, and Europe will never be Russian.

Form yourselves into a sworn brotherhood, to defend, not the empty conception of a Fatherland, but your homes, your wives, your children, and, with them, our future. In these hours, the whole German people looks to you, my fighters in the East, and only hopes that, thanks to your resolution and fanaticism, thanks to your weapons, and under your leadership, the Bolshevik assault will be choked in a bath of blood. At this moment, when Fate has removed from the earth the greatest war criminal of all time, the turning point of this war will be decided.

Signed: ADOLF HITLER

Extract from H R Trevor-Roper *Hitler's War Directives, 1939-1945* (London, 1964). Quoted by permission of Sidgwick & Jackson Limited.

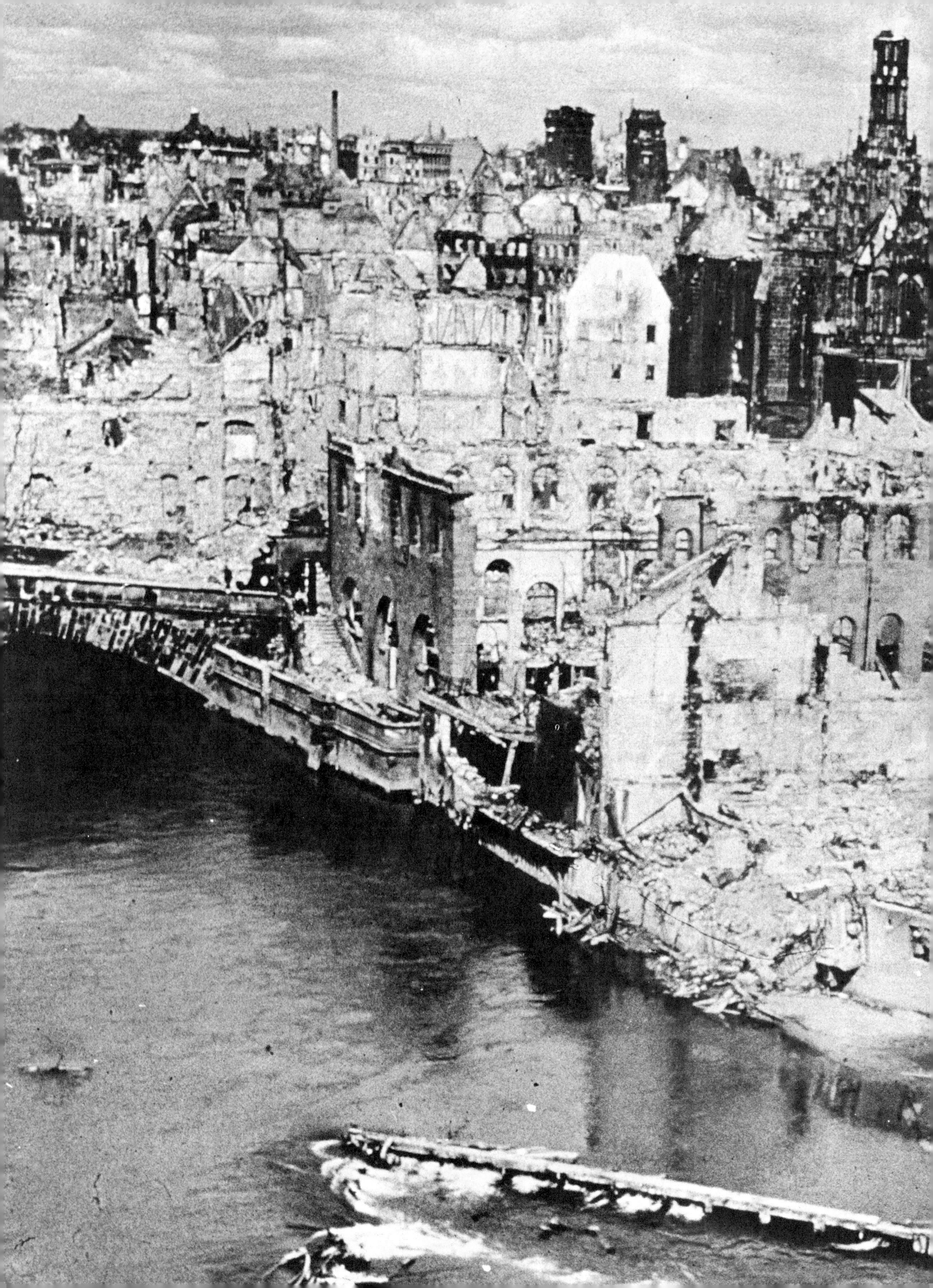

Below: **The remains of the walled city of Nuremberg, scene of Nazi rallies, after a series of Allied air raids.**

Top: **Dr Goebbels briefs the last defenders of Berlin. During the last months of the Third Reich he lived in the Bunker as part of Hitler's entourage.**
Above: **Heinrich Himmler visits some defenders of Berlin outside the city.**

began its final push it had at its disposal twice as many troops and artillery and three times as many armored vehicles as the Germans. In addition it had some 60,000 partisan irregulars helping it, absolute control in the air and plentiful gasoline supplies while the Germans were very short of fuel. Nevertheless the Germans fought well and Allied advance was slow. General Vietinghoff nonetheless saw the necessity of retiring behind the natural barrier of the river Po, but Hitler countermanded this order. By now Hitler's orders emanating from far away Berlin were generally disregarded and the Germans retreated just in time to avoid encirclement. On 26 April the Americans took Verona and the 8th Army penetrated the Venetian line. Italian partisan forces had blocked the Alpine passes so that the German Army in Italy was in reality trapped and at the mercy of Allied armies. In fact in February 1945 General Karl Wolff of the Waffen SS had opened negotiations with Allen Dulles (OSS Chief) in Switzerland about German surrender in Italy. However after the Allied offensive in April Himmler, who was kept informed, froze the negotiations. Still it was too late and the demoralized German troops were surrendering everywhere, although Wolff had negotiated surrender on 2 May 1945.

It was obvious that the last battle of the war would take place in the East and Hitler together with Himmler were feverishly preparing for it. It was at this desperate stage that Himmler and his SS finally took up the question of Soviet prisoners and decided to make use of them. As has been seen the Wehrmacht made use of these unfortunate captives in auxiliary capacity against Hitler's and Rosenberg's previous wishes. Pleading absolute military necessity some 3000 to 4000 Russians and Ukrainians made up every German division deployed in the East; often they had to fight, as many German divisions were practically devoid of German troops. However these hundreds of thousands of Russians and Ukrainians wanted to fight for their countries against the Stalinist régime rather than in the German armies. But the Wehrmacht, while recognizing their aims and respecting their desires,

Above: **The remains of an Me 109 at the Messerschmitt aircraft factory in Augsburg.**
Right: **Soviet artillery within Berlin fires at the Reichstag building.**

Left : **Soviet soldiers atop the Reichstag raise the hammer and sickle flag of Communism over the soon-to-be-divided city of Berlin.**
Right : **Berlin residents look for clothes and other essentials on a makeshift notice board (tree).**

never succeeded in persuading the politicians, especially Hitler, to enable them to fight their own battles.

In the summer of 1942, when General Andrey Vlasov was captured, the Russians even got themselves a capable organizer and leader who was willing to collaborate with the Germans in order to destroy the Stalinist régime with which he had become disillusioned. When previously the Smolensk Committee appealed to Hitler to raise a million-strong Russian National Liberation Army to fight against Stalin, he did not even bother to reply. Vlasov now took up this same cause and sponsored by the Wehrmacht he went round the prisoner of war camps, where he was received with certain enthusiasm. What was more significant were the requests of Soviet deserters, who as late as 1944 amounted to some 2500 to 3000 every day, to be enrolled in Vlasov's Liberation Army, which did not exist. Vlasov did impress Rosenberg who would have liked to help the Russian Liberation Movement, but as usual he failed to impress Hitler with his case, and therefore gave it up. However by 1943 Rosenberg was collaborating with Reichsführer SS Himmler and Himmler had more influence on Hitler than Rosenberg; in any case Himmler was prepared to go behind Hitler's back once he convinced himself that in the case of the Russian Liberation Movement, German national interests and his own coincided.

While the Wehrmacht, with the help of the Propaganda Ministry, could set up Vlasov and some 1200 propaganda specialists at Dahrendorf, Himmler could actually form these prisoners into military units and make them part of his Waffen SS. Quite cynically SS officers who saw fighting on the Eastern Front changed their ideas on the *Untermensch* theory and seeing the toughness and even enthusiasm of these *Untermenschen* recruited them for their SS units. Himmler swiftly gave permission and the SS recruited men from among the minor nationalities straight away and they quickly proved themselves to be as fanatical fighters as the SS themselves. Out of the 910,000 Waffen SS only 310,000 were Germans. The rest were non-Germans, mainly Slavs or "Germanic" volunteers. However by the fall of 1943 Hitler, who tolerated this "unofficial" recruitment, blamed the *Osttruppen* for minor Soviet successes on the Eastern Front, and insisted on having them all transferred to the West. Still seeing Hitler's acquiescence, the SS launched Operation *Skorpion* in the spring of 1944. Large Russian units were organized by the SS on the southern sector of the Eastern Front and the SS Standartenführer d'Alquen even wanted to issue a political declaration of the Russian Liberation movement. Though he was unable to do

Left : **Captured German general officers in front of the ruins of the Reichstag. It has since been restored by the East Germans.**
Right : **Soviet tanks enter Berlin in the final days of the Third Reich. Fighting more or less ceased on 2 May 1945.**